**Anglican—Roman Catholic
International Commission**

THE FINAL REPORT

Windsor, September 1981

CTS/SPCK

D0191888

First published in Great Britain 1982
SPCK, Holy Trinity Church, Marylebone Road, London NW1 4DU
Catholic Truth Society, 38—40 Eccleston Square, London SW1V 1PD
Seventh impression 1985

The Final Report of the Anglican—Roman Catholic International
Commission includes copyright material previously published as
follows:

> An Agreed Statement on Eucharistic Doctrine 1972
> Ministry and Ordination 1973
> The Agreed Statements 1975
> Authority in the Church 1977
> The Three Agreed Statements 1978
> Elucidations: Eucharistic Doctrine,
> Ministry and Ordination 1979

The Malta Report of the Joint Preparatory Commission was published
in *Anglican/Roman Catholic Dialogue: The Work of the Preparatory
Commission*, ed. Alan C. Clark and Colin Davey, 1974.

The Common Declarations of 1966 and 1977 have been published in
various places.

Printed in Great Britain by
Bocardo & Church Army Press Ltd., Cowley, Oxford

ISBN 0 281 03859 7   (SPCK)
       0 85183 451 5   (CTS)

Contents

Preface to the Final Report

The Report which follows is the outcome of work begun at Gazzada, Italy, on 9 January 1967. A Joint Preparatory Commission met there, in fulfilment of a joint decision by Pope Paul VI and Archbishop Michael Ramsey, expressed in a Common Declaration during their meeting in Rome in March 1966. Meeting three times in less than a year, that Commission produced a Report which registered considerable areas of Roman Catholic—Anglican agreement, pointed to persisting historical differences and outlined a programme of 'growing together' which should include, though not be exhausted in, serious dialogue on these differences. It proclaimed penitence for the past, thankfulness for the graces of the present, urgency and resolve for a future in which our common aim would be the restoration of full organic unity.

That Report was endorsed in substance by a letter of Cardinal Bea in June 1968 and by the Lambeth Conference a few weeks later. In January 1970 the signatories of the present Report met first as 'The Anglican—Roman Catholic International Commission'. Eight members of the Preparatory Commission continued to serve on the new Commission.

The purpose of this Preface is to explain briefly the aim and methods of ARCIC as these have matured in the light of our own experience, of the developments—in some aspects rapid—within our own Churches in the twelve years of our experience, in response to criticisms we have received and having regard to other ecumenical dialogues.

From the beginning we were determined, in accordance with our mandate, and in the spirit of Phil.3.13, 'forgetting what lies behind and straining forward to what lies ahead', to discover each other's faith as it is today and to appeal to history only for enlightenment, not as a way of perpetuating past controversy. In putting this resolve into practice we learned as we progressed. As early as 1970 our preliminary papers on our three main topics link each of them with 'the Church', and this perspective was maintained and is reflected in what follows here: our work is introduced with a statement on the Church, building on the concept of *koinonia*. In the Statement *Eucharistic Doctrine* (Windsor 1971) we went so far as to claim 'substantial agreement' which is consistent with 'a variety of theological approaches within both our communions'. The Preface to our Statement *Ministry and Ordination* (Canterbury 1973) expressed the belief 'that in what we have said here both Anglicans and Roman Catholics will recognize their own faith'.

It was in the first of our two Statements on Authority (*Authority in the Church I*, Venice 1976) that we spoke more fully and revealed a more developed awareness of our aims and methods. Because 'it was precisely in the problem of papal primacy that our historical divisions found their unhappy origin', reference was made to the 'distinction between the ideal and the actual which is important for the reading of our document and for the understanding of the method we have used' (Authority I, Preface). Acknowledging the growing convergence of method and outlook of theologians in our two traditions, we emphasized our avoidance of the emotive language of past polemics and our seeking to pursue *together* that restatement of doctrine which new times and conditions are, as we both recognize, regularly calling for (Authority I, para. 25). In concluding we felt already able to invite our authorities to consider whether our Statements expressed a unity at the level of faith sufficient to call for 'closer sharing . . . in life, worship, and mission'.

Some provisional response to this was forthcoming a few months later in the *Common Declaration* of Pope Paul VI and Archbishop Donald Coggan, made during the latter's visit to Rome in April 1977. Echoing our original statement of intent, 'the restoration of complete communion in faith and sacramental life', Pope and Archbishop declared, 'Our call to this is one with the sublime Christian vocation itself, which is a call to communion' (cf. 1 John 1.3). This passage (*Common Declaration*, paras. 8—9) provides a striking endorsement of a central theme of our Statements, and insists that though our communion remains imperfect it 'stands at the centre of our witness to the world'. 'Our divisions hinder this witness, but they do not close all roads we may travel together.' In other words, the *koinonia* which is the governing concept of what follows here is not a static concept—it demands movement forward, perfecting. We need to accept its implications.

This official encouragement has been echoed by many of our critics. We have seen all of them, encouraging or not, as reflecting the interest aroused by the dialogue and helping us to make ourselves clearer, as we have tried to do in the *Elucidations* (Salisbury 1979 and Windsor 1981).

Paragraph 24 of our Statement *Authority in the Church I* made it clear that, while we had reached a high degree of agreement on 'authority in the Church and in particular on the basic principles of primacy', differences persisted concerning papal authority. A much closer examination of those differences has been our main task since then. The results of that work are embodied in the Statement *Authority in the Church II* (Windsor 1981) which is here presented for the first time. Though much of the material in this Final Report has been published earlier, we are confident that the Report will be read as a whole, and that particular sentences or passages will not be taken out of context.

We believe that growing numbers in both our communions accept that, in the words of the Second Vatican Council's *Decree on Ecumenism*, 'There can be no ecumenism worthy of the name without interior conversion. For it is from newness of attitudes of mind, from self-denial and unstinted love, that desires of unity take their rise and develop in a mature way' (*Unitatis Redintegratio*, para. 7).

It would be wrong, however, to suggest that all the criticisms we have received over the twelve years of our work have been encouraging. We are aware of the limits of our work—that it is a service to the people of God, and needs to find acceptance among them.

But we have as much reason now as ever to echo the concluding lines of the *Common Declaration* of 1977:

to be baptized into Christ is to be baptized into hope—'and hope does not disappoint us because God's love has been poured into our hearts through the Holy Spirit which has been given us' (Rom. 5.5). Christian hope manifests itself in prayer and action—in prudence but also in courage. We pledge ourselves and exhort the faithful of the Roman Catholic Church and of the Anglican Communion to live and work courageously in this hope of reconciliation and unity in our common Lord.

Introduction

1   Our two communions have been separated for over 400 years. This separation, involving serious doctrinal differences, has been aggravated by theological polemics and mutual intolerance, which have reached into and affected many departments of life. Nevertheless, although our unity has been impaired through separation, it has not been destroyed. Many bonds still unite us: we confess the same faith in the one true God; we have received the same Spirit; we have been baptized with the same baptism; and we preach the same Christ.

2   Controversy between our two communions has centred on the eucharist, on the meaning and function of ordained ministry, and on the nature and exercise of authority in the Church. Although we are not yet in full communion, what the Commission has done has convinced us that substantial agreement on these divisive issues is now possible.

3   In producing these Statements, we have been concerned, not to evade the difficulties, but rather to avoid the controversial language in which they have often been discussed. We have taken seriously the issues that have divided us, and have sought solutions by re-examining our common inheritance, particularly the Scriptures.

4   The subjects which we were required to consider as a result of the Report of the Joint Preparatory Commission all relate to the true nature of the Church. Fundamental to all our Statements is the concept of *koinonia* (communion). In the early Christian tradition, reflection on the experience of *koinonia* opened the way to the understanding of the mystery of the Church. Although '*koinonia*' is never equated with 'Church' in the New Testament, it is the

term that most aptly expresses the mystery underlying the various New Testament images of the Church. When, for example, the Church is called the people of the new covenant or the bride of Christ, the context is primarily that of communion. Although such images as the Temple, the new Jerusalem, or the royal priesthood may carry institutional overtones, their primary purpose is to depict the Church's experience as a partaking in the salvation of Christ. When the Church is described as the body of Christ, the household of God, or the holy nation, the emphasis is upon the relationships among its members as well as upon their relationship with Christ the Head.

5   Union with God in Christ Jesus through the Spirit is the heart of Christian *koinonia*. Among the various ways in which the term *koinonia* is used in different New Testament contexts, we concentrate on that which signifies a relation between persons resulting from their participation in one and the same reality (cf. 1 John 1.3). The Son of God has taken to himself our human nature, and he has sent upon us his Spirit, who makes us so truly members of the body of Christ that we too are able to call God 'Abba, Father' (Rom. 8.15; Gal. 4.6). Moreover, sharing in the same Holy Spirit, whereby we become members of the same body of Christ and adopted children of the same Father, we are also bound to one another in a completely new relationship. *Koinonia* with one another is entailed by our *koinonia* with God in Christ. This is the mystery of the Church.

6   This theme of *koinonia* runs through our Statements. In them we present the eucharist as the effectual sign of *koinonia*, *episcope* as serving the *koinonia*, and primacy as a visible link and focus of *koinonia*.

In the Statement *Eucharistic Doctrine* the eucharist is seen as the sacrament of Christ, by which he builds up and nurtures his people in the *koinonia* of his body. By the eucharist all the baptized are brought into communion with the source of *koinonia*. He is the one who destroyed the walls dividing humanity (Eph. 2.14); he is the one who died to gather into unity all the children of God his Father (cf. John 11.52; 17.20ff).

In the Statement *Ministry and Ordination* it is made clear that *episcope* exists only to serve *koinonia*. The ordained minister presiding at the eucharist is a sign of Christ gathering his people and giving them his body and blood. The Gospel he preaches is the Gospel of unity. Through the ministry of word and sacrament the Holy Spirit is given for the building up of the body of Christ. It is the responsibility of those exercising *episcope* to enable all the people to use the gifts of the Spirit which they have received for the enrichment of the Church's common life. It is also their responsibility to keep the community under the law of Christ in mutual love and in concern for others; for the reconciled community of the Church has been given the ministry of reconciliation (2 Cor. 5.18).

In both Statements on authority the Commission, discussing primacy, sees it as a necessary link between all those exercising *episcope* within the *koinonia*. All ministers of the Gospel need to be in communion with one another, for the one Church is a communion of local churches. They also need to be united in the apostolic faith. Primacy, as a focus within the *koinonia*, is an assurance that what they teach and do is in accord with the faith of the apostles.

7 The Church as *koinonia* requires visible expression because it is intended to be the 'sacrament' of God's saving work. A sacrament is both sign and instrument. The *koinonia* is a sign that God's purpose in Christ is being realized in the world by grace. It is also an instrument for the accomplishment of this purpose, inasmuch as it proclaims the truth of the Gospel and witnesses to it by its

life, thus entering more deeply into the mystery of the Kingdom. The community thus announces what it is called to become.

8   The *koinonia* is grounded in the word of God preached, believed and obeyed. Through this word the saving work of God is proclaimed. In the fullness of time this salvation was realized in the person of Jesus, the Word of God incarnate. Jesus prepared his followers to receive through the Holy Spirit the fruit of his death and resurrection, the culmination of his life of obedience, and to become the heralds of salvation. In the New Testament it is clear that the community is established by a baptism inseparable from faith and conversion, that its mission is to proclaim the Gospel of God, and that its common life is sustained by the eucharist. This remains the pattern for the Christian Church. The Church is the community of those reconciled with God and with each other because it is the community of those who believe in Jesus Christ and are justified through God's grace. It is also the reconciling community, because it has been called to bring to all mankind, through the preaching of the Gospel, God's gracious offer of redemption.

9   Christ's will and prayer are that his disciples should be one. Those who have received the same word of God and have been baptized in the same Spirit cannot, without disobedience, acquiesce in a state of separation. Unity is of the essence of the Church, and since the Church is visible its unity also must be visible. Full visible communion between our two Churches cannot be achieved without mutual recognition of sacraments and ministry, together with the common acceptance of a universal primacy, at one with the episcopal college in the service of the *koinonia*.

Eucharistic Doctrine

Co-Chairmen's Preface

The following Agreed Statement evolved from the thinking and the discussion of the Anglican—Roman Catholic International Commission over the past two years. The result has been a conviction among members of the Commission that we have reached agreement on essential points of eucharistic doctrine. We are equally convinced ourselves that, though no attempt was made to present a fully comprehensive treatment of the subject, nothing essential has been omitted. The document, agreed upon at our third meeting, at Windsor, on 7 September 1971, has been presented to our official authorities, but obviously it cannot be ratified by them until such time as our respective Churches can evaluate its conclusions.

We would want to point out that the members of the Commission who subscribed to this Statement have been officially appointed and come from many countries, representing a wide variety of theological background. Our intention was to reach a consensus at the level of faith, so that all of us might be able to say, within the limits of the Statement: this is the Christian faith of the Eucharist.

September 1971

H. R. McADOO
ALAN C. CLARK

The Statement (1971)

Introduction

1 In the course of the Church's history several traditions have developed in expressing Christian understanding of the eucharist. (For example, various names have become customary as descriptions of the eucharist: Lord's supper, liturgy, holy mysteries, synaxis, mass, holy communion. The eucharist has become the most universally accepted term.) An important stage in progress towards organic unity is a substantial consensus on the purpose and meaning of the eucharist. Our intention has been to seek a deeper understanding of the reality of the eucharist which is consonant with biblical teaching and with the tradition of our common inheritance, and to express in this document the consensus we have reached.

2 Through the life, death and resurrection of Jesus Christ God has reconciled men to himself, and in Christ he offers unity to all mankind. By his word God calls us into a new relationship with himself as our Father and with one another as his children—a relationship inaugurated by baptism into Christ through the Holy Spirit, nurtured and deepened through the eucharist, and expressed in a confession of one faith and a common life of loving service.

I *The Mystery of the Eucharist*

3 When his people are gathered at the eucharist to commemorate his saving acts for our redemption, Christ makes effective among us the eternal benefits of his victory and elicits and renews our response of faith, thanksgiving and self-surrender. Christ through the Holy Spirit in the eucharist builds up the life of the Church, strengthens its fellowship and furthers its mission. The identity of the

Church as the body of Christ is both expressed and effectively proclaimed by its being centred in, and partaking of, his body and blood. In the whole action of the eucharist, and in and by his sacramental presence given through bread and wine, the crucified and risen Lord, according to his promise, offers himself to his people.

4 In the eucharist we proclaim the Lord's death until he comes. Receiving a foretaste of the kingdom to come, we look back with thanksgiving to what Christ has done for us, we greet him present among us, we look forward to his final appearing in the fullness of his kingdom when 'The Son also himself (shall) be subject unto him that put all things under him, that God may be all in all' (1 Cor. 15.28). When we gather around the same table in this communal meal at the invitation of the same Lord and when we 'partake of the one loaf', we are one in commitment not only to Christ and to one another, but also to the mission of the Church in the world.

II *The Eucharist and the Sacrifice of Christ*

5 Christ's redeeming death and resurrection took place once and for all in history. Christ's death on the cross, the culmination of his whole life of obedience, was the one, perfect and sufficient sacrifice for the sins of the world. There can be no repetition of or addition to what was then accomplished once for all by Christ. Any attempt to express a nexus between the sacrifice of Christ and the eucharist must not obscure this fundamental fact of the Christian faith.[1] Yet God has given the eucharist to his

---

[1] The early Church in expressing the meaning of Christ's death and resurrection often used the language of sacrifice. For the Hebrew *sacrifice* was a traditional means of communication with God. The passover, for example, was a communal meal; the day of atonement was essentially expiatory; and the covenant established communion between God and man.

Church as a means through which the atoning work of Christ on the cross is proclaimed and made effective in the life of the Church. The notion of *memorial* as understood in the passover celebration at the time of Christ—i.e. the making effective in the present of an event in the past—has opened the way to a clearer understanding of the relationship between Christ's sacrifice and the eucharist. The eucharistic memorial is no mere calling to mind of a past event or of its significance, but the Church's effectual proclamation of God's mighty acts. Christ instituted the eucharist as a memorial (*anamnesis*) of the totality of God's reconciling action in him. In the eucharistic prayer the church continues to make a perpetual memorial of Christ's death, and his members, united with God and one another, give thanks for all his mercies, entreat the benefits of his passion on behalf of the whole Church, participate in these benefits and enter into the movement of his self-offering.

III   *The Presence of Christ*

6   Communion with Christ in the eucharist presupposes his true presence, effectually signified by the bread and wine which, in this mystery, become his body and blood.[2] The real presence of his body and blood can, however, only be understood within the context of the redemptive activity whereby he gives himself, and in himself reconciliation, peace and life, to his own. On the one hand, the eucharistic gift springs out of the paschal mystery of Christ's death and resurrection, in which God's saving

---

[2] The word *transubstantiation* is commonly used in the Roman Catholic Church to indicate that God acting in the eucharist effects a change in the inner reality of the elements. The term should be seen as affirming the *fact* of Christ's presence and of the mysterious and radical change which takes place. In contemporary Roman Catholic theology it is not understood as explaining *how* the change takes place.

14

purpose has already been definitively realized. On the other hand, its purpose is to transmit the life of the crucified and risen Christ to his body, the Church, so that its members may be more fully united with Christ and with one another.

7 Christ is present and active, in various ways, in the entire eucharistic celebration. It is the same Lord who through the proclaimed word invites his people to his table, who through his minister presides at that table, and who gives himself sacramentally in the body and blood of his paschal sacrifice. It is the Lord present at the right hand of the Father, and therefore transcending the sacramental order, who thus offers to his Church, in the eucharistic signs, the special gift of himself.

8 The sacramental body and blood of the Saviour are present as an offering to the believer awaiting his welcome. When this offering is met by faith, a lifegiving encounter results. Through faith Christ's presence—which does not depend on the individual's faith in order to be the Lord's real gift of himself to his Church—becomes no longer just a presence *for* the believer, but also a presence *with* him. Thus, in considering the mystery of the eucharistic presence, we must recognize both the sacramental sign of Christ's presence and the personal relationship between Christ and the faithful which arises from that presence.

9 The Lord's words at the last supper, 'Take and eat; this is my body', do not allow us to dissociate the gift of the presence and the act of sacramental eating. The elements are not mere signs; Christ's body and blood become really present and are really given. But they are really present and given in order that, receiving them, believers may be united in communion with Christ the Lord.

10 According to the traditional order of the liturgy the

consecratory prayer (*anaphora*) leads to the communion of the faithful. Through this prayer of thanksgiving, a word of faith addressed to the Father, the bread and wine become the body and blood of Christ by the action of the Holy Spirit, so that in communion we eat the flesh of Christ and drink his blood.

11 The Lord who thus comes to his people in the power of the Holy Spirit is the Lord of glory. In the eucharistic celebration we anticipate the joys of the age to come. By the transforming action of the Spirit of God, earthly bread and wine become the heavenly manna and the new wine, the eschatological banquet for the new man: elements of the first creation become pledges and first fruits of the new heaven and the new earth.

Conclusion

12 We believe that we have reached substantial agreement on the doctrine of the eucharist. Although we are all conditioned by the traditional ways in which we have expressed and practised our eucharistic faith, we are convinced that if there are any remaining points of disagreement they can be resolved on the principles here established. We acknowledge a variety of theological approaches within both our communions. But we have seen it as our task to find a way of advancing together beyond the doctrinal disagreements of the past. It is our hope that, in view of the agreement which we have reached on eucharistic faith, this doctrine will no longer constitute an obstacle to the unity we seek.

Elucidation (1979)

1 When each of the Agreed Statements was published, the Commission invited and has received comment and criticism. This *Elucidation* is an attempt to expand and explain to those who have responded some points raised in connection with *Eucharistic Doctrine* (Windsor 1971).

Substantial Agreement

2 The Commission was not asked to produce a comprehensive treatise on the eucharist, but only to examine differences which in the controversies of the past divided our two communions. The aim of the Commission has been to see whether we can today discover substantial agreement in faith on the eucharist. Questions have been asked about the meaning of *substantial* agreement. It means that the document represents not only the judgement of all its members—i.e. it is an agreement—but their unanimous agreement 'on essential matters where it considers that doctrine admits no divergence' (Ministry, para. 17)—i.e. it is a substantial agreement. Members of the Commission are united in their conviction 'that if there are any remaining points of disagreement they can be resolved on the principles here established' (Eucharist, para. 12).

Comments and Criticisms

3 The following comments and criticisms are representative of the many received and are considered by the Commission to be of particular importance.

In spite of the firm assertion made in the Agreed Statement of the 'once for all' nature of Christ's sacrifice, some have still been anxious that the term *anamnesis* may conceal the reintroduction of the theory of a repeated immolation. Others have suspected that the word refers

17

not only to the historical events of salvation but also to an eternal sacrifice in heaven. Others again have doubted whether *anamnesis* sufficiently implies the reality indicated by traditional sacrificial language concerning the eucharist. Moreover, the accuracy and adequacy of the Commission's exegesis of *anamnesis* have been questioned.

Some critics have been unhappy about the realistic language used in this Agreed Statement, and have questioned such words as *become* and *change*. Others have wondered whether the permanence of Christ's eucharistic presence has been sufficiently acknowledged, with a consequent request for a discussion of the reserved sacrament and devotions associated with it. Similarly there have been requests for clarification of the Commission's attitude to receptionism.

4   Behind these criticisms there lies a profound but often unarticulated anxiety that the Commission has been using new theological language which evades unresolved differences. Related to this anxiety is the further question as to the nature of the agreement claimed by the Commission. Does the language of the Commission conceal an ambiguity (either intentional or unintentional) in language which enables members of the two churches to see their own faith in the Agreed Statement without having in fact reached a genuine consensus?

Anamnesis and Sacrifice

5   The Commission has been criticized for its use of the term *anamnesis*. It chose the word used in New Testament accounts of the institution of the eucharist at the last supper:

'Do this as a memorial (*anamnesin*) of me' (1 Cor. 11.24–25; Luke 22.19: JB, NEB).

The word is also to be found in Justin Martyr in the second century. Recalling the last supper he writes:

'Jesus, taking bread and having given thanks, said, "Do this for my memorial (*anamnesin*): This is my body"; and likewise, taking the cup, and giving thanks, he said, "This is my blood" ' (*First Apology* 66; cf. *Dialogue with Trypho* 117).

From this time onwards the term is found at the very heart of the eucharistic prayers of both East and West, not only in the institution narrative but also in the prayer which follows and elsewhere: cf. e.g. The Liturgy of St John Chrysostom; Eucharistic Prayer I—The Roman Missal; The Order of the Administration of the Lord's Supper or Holy Communion—The Book of Common Prayer (1662); and Rites A and B of the Church of England Alternative Service Book (1980).

The word is also found in patristic and later theology. The Council of Trent in explaining the relation between the sacrifice of the cross and the eucharist uses the words *commemoratio* and *memoria* (Session 22, ch. 1); and in the Book of Common Prayer (1662) the Catechism states that the sacrament of the Lord's Supper was ordained 'for the continual *remembrance* of the sacrifice of the death of Christ, and of the benefits which we receive thereby'. The frequent use of the term in contemporary theology is illustrated by *One Baptism One Eucharist and a Mutually Recognized Ministry* (Faith and Order Commission Paper No. 73), as well as by the *General Instruction on the Roman Missal* (1970).

The Commission believes that the traditional understanding of sacramental reality, in which the once-for-all event of salvation becomes effective in the present through the action of the Holy Spirit, is well expressed by the word *anamnesis*. We accept this use of the word which seems to do full justice to the semitic background. Furthermore it enables us to affirm a strong conviction of sacramental realism and to reject mere symbolism. However the selection of this word by the Commission does not mean that our common eucharistic faith may not be expressed in other terms.

In the exposition of the Christian doctrine of redemption the word *sacrifice* has been used in two intimately associated ways. In the New Testament, sacrificial language refers primarily to the historical events of Christ's saving work for us. The tradition of the Church, as evidenced for example in its liturgies, used similar language to designate in the eucharistic celebration the *anamnesis* of this historical event. Therefore it is possible to say at the same time that there is only one unrepeatable sacrifice in the historical sense, but that the eucharist is a sacrifice in the sacramental sense, provided that it is clear that this is not a repetition of the historical sacrifice.

There is therefore one historical, unrepeatable sacrifice, offered once for all by Christ and accepted once for all by the Father. In the celebration of the memorial, Christ in the Holy Spirit unites his people with himself in a sacramental way so that the Church enters into the movement of his self-offering. In consequence, even though the Church is active in this celebration, this adds nothing to the efficacy of Christ's sacrifice upon the cross, because the action is itself the fruit of this sacrifice. The Church in celebrating the eucharist gives thanks for the gift of Christ's sacrifice and identifies itself with the will of Christ who has offered himself to the Father on behalf of all mankind.

Christ's Presence in the Eucharist

6   Criticism has been evoked by the statement that the bread and wine become the body and blood of Christ in the eucharist (para. 10). The word *become* has been suspected of expressing a materialistic conception of Christ's

presence, and this has seemed to some to be confirmed in the footnote on the word *transubstantiation* which also speaks of *change*. It is feared that this suggests that Christ's presence in the eucharist is confined to the elements, and that the Real Presence involves a physical change in them.

In order to respond to these comments the Commission recalls that the Statement affirmed that:

(*a*) It is the glorified Lord himself whom the community of the faithful encounters in the eucharistic celebration through the preaching of the word, in the fellowship of the Lord's supper, in the heart of the believer, and, in a sacramental way, through the gifts of his body and blood, already given on the cross for their salvation.

(*b*) His body and blood are given through the action of the Holy Spirit, appropriating bread and wine so that they become the food of the new creation already inaugurated by the coming of Christ (cf. paras. 7, 10, 11).

Becoming does not here imply material change. Nor does the liturgical use of the word imply that the bread and wine become Christ's body and blood in such a way that in the eucharistic celebration his presence is limited to the consecrated elements. It does not imply that Christ becomes present in the eucharist in the same manner that he was present in his earthly life. It does not imply that this *becoming* follows the physical laws of this world. What is here affirmed is a sacramental presence in which God uses realities of this world to convey the realities of the new creation: bread for this life becomes the bread of eternal life. Before the eucharistic prayer, to the question: 'What is that?', the believer answers: 'It is bread.' After the eucharistic prayer, to the same question he answers: 'It is truly the body of Christ, the Bread of Life.'

In the sacramental order the realities of faith become present in visible and tangible signs, enabling Christians to avail themselves of the fruits of the once-for-all redemption. In the eucharist the human person encounters in faith the person of Christ in his sacramental body and blood. This is the sense in which the community, the body of Christ, by partaking of the sacramental body of the risen Lord, grows into the unity God intends for his Church. The ultimate change intended by God is the transformation of human beings into the likeness of Christ. The bread and wine *become* the sacramental body and blood of Christ in order that the Christian community may *become* more truly what it already is, the body of Christ.

Gift and Reception

7   This transformation into the likeness of Christ requires that the eucharistic gifts be received in faith. In the mystery of the eucharist we discern not one but two complementary movements within an indissoluble unity: Christ giving his body and blood, and the communicants feeding upon them in their hearts by faith. Some traditions have placed a special emphasis on the association of Christ's presence with the consecrated elements; others have emphasized Christ's presence in the heart of the believer through reception by faith. In the past, acute difficulties have arisen when one or other of these emphases has become almost exclusive. In the opinion of the Commission neither emphasis is incompatible with eucharistic faith, provided that the complementary movement emphasized by the other position is not denied. Eucharistic doctrine must hold together these two movements since in the eucharist, the sacrament of the New Covenant, Christ gives himself to his people so that they may receive him through faith.

Reservation

8   The practice of reserving the sacrament for reception after the congregation has dispersed is known to date back to the second century (cf. Justin Martyr, *First Apology*, 65 and 67). In so far as it maintains the complementary movements already referred to (as for example, when communion is taken to the sick) this practice clearly accords with the purpose of the institution of the eucharist. But later there developed a tendency to stress the veneration of Christ's presence in the consecrated elements. In some places this tendency became so pronounced that the original purpose of reservation was in danger of becoming totally obscured. If veneration is wholly dissociated from the eucharistic celebration of the community it contradicts the true doctrine of the eucharist.

Consideration of this question requires clarification of the understanding of the eucharist. Adoration in the celebration of the eucharist is first and foremost offered to the Father. It is to lead us to the Father that Christ unites us to himself through our receiving of his body and blood. The Christ whom we adore in the eucharist is Christ glorifying his Father. The movement of all our adoration is to the Father, through, with, and in Christ, in the power of the Spirit.

The whole eucharistic action is a continuous movement in which Christ offers himself in his sacramental body and blood to his people and in which they receive him in faith and thanksgiving. Consequently communion administered from the reserved sacrament to those unable to attend the eucharistic celebration is rightly understood as an extension of that celebration. Differences arise between those who would practise reservation for this reason only, and those who would also regard it as a means of eucharistic devotion. For the latter, adoration of Christ in the reserved sacrament should be regarded as an extension of eucharistic worship, even though it does not include immediate sacramental reception, which remains the primary purpose of reservation (cf. the Instruction *Eucharisticum Mysterium*, para. 49, of the Sacred Congregation of Rites (AAS 59, 1967)). Any dissociation of such devotion from this primary purpose, which is communion in Christ of all his members, is a distortion in eucharistic practice.

9   In spite of this clarification, others still find any kind of adoration of Christ in the reserved sacrament unacceptable. They believe that it is in fact impossible in such a practice truly to hold together the two movements of which we have spoken: and that this devotion can hardly fail to produce such an emphasis upon the association of Christ's sacramental presence with the consecrated bread and wine as to suggest too static and localized a presence that disrupts the movement as well as the balance of the whole eucharistic action (cf. Article 28 of the Articles of Religion).

That there can be a divergence in matters of practice and in theological judgements relating to them, without destroying a common eucharistic faith, illustrates what we mean by *substantial* agreement. Differences of theology and practice may well coexist with a real consensus on the essentials of eucharistic faith—as in fact they do within each of our communions.

Other Issues

10   Concern has been expressed that we have said nothing about intercommunion, though claiming to have attained a substantial agreement on eucharistic faith. The reason is that we are agreed that a responsible judgement on this matter cannot be made on the basis of this

Statement alone, because intercommunion also involves issues relating to authority and to the mutual recognition of ministry. There are other important issues, such as the eschatological dimension of the eucharist and its relation to contemporary questions of human liberation and social justice, which we have either not fully developed or not explicitly treated. These are matters which call for the common attention of our churches, but they are not a source of division between us and are therefore outside our mandate.

Ministry and Ordination

Co-Chairmen's Preface

At Windsor, in 1971, the Anglican—Roman Catholic International Commission was able to achieve an Agreed Statement on Eucharistic Doctrine. In accordance with the programme adopted at Venice in 1970, we have now, at our meeting in Canterbury in 1973, turned our attention to the doctrine of ministry, specifically to our understanding of the ordained ministry and its place in the life of the Church. The present document is the result of the work of this officially appointed Commission and is offered to our authorities for their consideration. At this stage it remains an agreed statement of the Commission and no more.

We acknowledge with gratitude our debt to the many studies and discussions which have treated the same material. While respecting the different forms that ministry has taken in other traditions, we hope that the clarification of our understanding expressed in the statement will be of service to them also.

We have submitted the statement, therefore, to our authorities and, with their authorization, we publish it as a document of the Commission with a view to its discussion. Even though there may be differences of emphasis within our two traditions, yet we believe that in what we have said here both Anglican and Roman Catholic will recognize their own faith.

September 1973

H. R. McADOO

ALAN C. CLARK

The Statement (1973)

Introduction

1 Our intention has been to seek a deeper understanding of ministry which is consonant with biblical teaching and with the traditions of our common inheritance, and to express in this document the consensus we have reached.[1] This Statement is not designed to be an exhaustive treatment of ministry. It seeks to express our basic agreement in the doctrinal areas that have been the source of controversy between us, in the wider context of our common convictions about the ministry.

2 Within the Roman Catholic Church and the Anglican Communion there exists a diversity of forms of ministerial service. Of more specific ways of service, while some are undertaken without particular initiative from official authority, others may receive a mandate from ecclesiastical authorities. The ordained ministry can only be rightly understood within this broader context of various ministries, all of which are the work of one and the same Spirit.

I Ministry in the Life of the Church

3 The life and self-offering of Christ perfectly express what it is to serve God and man. All Christian ministry, whose purpose is always to build up the community (*koinonia*), flows and takes its shape from this source and model. The communion of men with God (and with each other) requires their reconciliation. This reconciliation, accomplished by the death and resurrection of Jesus Christ, is being realized in the life of the Church through the response of faith. While the Church is still in process of

---

[1] Cf. Eucharist, para. 1, which similarly speaks of a consensus reached with regard to the eucharist.

sanctification, its mission is nevertheless to be the instrument by which this reconciliation in Christ is proclaimed, his love manifested, and the means of salvation offered to men.

4   In the early Church the apostles exercised a ministry which remains of fundamental significance for the Church of all ages. It is difficult to deduce, from the New Testament use of 'apostle' for the Twelve, Paul, and others, a precise portrait of an apostle, but two primary features of the original apostolate are clearly discernible: a special relationship with the historical Christ, and a commission from him to the Church and the world (Matt. 28.19; Mark 3.14). All Christian apostolate originates in the sending of the Son by the Father. The Church is apostolic not only because its faith and life must reflect the witness to Jesus Christ given in the early Church by the apostles, but also because it is charged to continue in the apostles' commission to communicate to the world what it has received. Within the whole history of mankind the Church is to be the community of reconciliation.

5   All ministries are used by the Holy Spirit for the building up of the Church to be this reconciling community for the glory of God and the salvation of men (Eph. 4. 11–13). Within the New Testament ministerial actions are varied and functions not precisely defined. Explicit emphasis is given to the proclamation of the word and the preservation of apostolic doctrine, the care of the flock, and the example of Christian living. At least by the time of the Pastoral Epistles and 1 Peter, some ministerial functions are discernible in a more exact form. The evidence suggests that with the growth of the Church the importance of certain functions led to their being located in specific officers of the community. Since the Church is built up by the Holy Spirit primarily but not exclusively

31

through these ministerial functions, some form of recognition and authorization is already required in the New Testament period for those who exercise them in the name of Christ. Here we can see elements which will remain at the heart of what today we call ordination.

6   The New Testament shows that ministerial office played an essential part in the life of the Church in the first century, and we believe that the provision of a ministry of this kind is part of God's design for his people. Normative principles governing the purpose and function of the ministry are already present in the New Testament documents (e.g. Mark 10.43—5; Acts 20.28; 1 Tim. 4.12—16; 1 Pet. 5.1—4). The early churches may well have had considerable diversity in the structure of pastoral ministry, though it is clear that some churches were headed by ministers who were called *episcopoi* and *presbyteroi*. While the first missionary churches were not a loose aggregation of autonomous communities, we have no evidence that 'bishops' and 'presbyters' were appointed everywhere in the primitive period. The terms 'bishop' and 'presbyter' could be applied to the same man or to men with identical or very similar functions. Just as the formation of the canon of the New Testament was a process incomplete until the second half of the second century, so also the full emergence of the threefold ministry of bishop, presbyter, and deacon required a longer period than the apostolic age. Thereafter this threefold structure became universal in the Church.

II   *The Ordained Ministry*

7   The Christian community exists to give glory to God through the fulfilment of the Father's purpose. All Christians are called to serve this purpose by their life of prayer and surrender to divine grace, and by their careful

attention to the needs of all human beings. They should witness to God's compassion for all mankind and his concern for justice in the affairs of men. They should offer themselves to God in praise and worship, and devote their energies to bringing men into the fellowship of Christ's people, and so under his rule of love. The goal of the ordained ministry is to serve this priesthood of all the faithful. Like any human community the Church requires a focus of leadership and unity, which the Holy Spirit provides in the ordained ministry. This ministry assumes various patterns to meet the varying needs of those whom the Church is seeking to serve, and it is the role of the minister to co-ordinate the activities of the Church's fellowship and to promote what is necessary and useful for the Church's life and mission. He is to discern what is of the Spirit in the diversity of the Church's life and promote its unity.

8   In the New Testament a variety of images is used to describe the functions of this minister. He is servant, both of Christ and of the Church. As herald and ambassador he is an authoritative representative of Christ and proclaims his message of reconciliation. As teacher he explains and applies the word of God to the community. As shepherd he exercises pastoral care and guides the flock. He is a steward who may only provide for the household of God what belongs to Christ. He is to be an example both in holiness and in compassion.

9   An essential element in the ordained ministry is its responsibility for 'oversight' (*episcope*). This responsibility involves fidelity to the apostolic faith, its embodiment in the life of the Church today, and its transmission to the Church of tomorrow. Presbyters are joined with the bishop in his oversight of the church and in the ministry of the word and the sacraments; they are given authority to

preside at the eucharist and to pronounce absolution. Deacons, although not so empowered, are associated with bishops and presbyters in the ministry of word and sacrament, and assist in oversight.

10   Since the ordained ministers are ministers of the Gospel, every facet of their oversight is linked with the word of God. In the original mission and witness recorded in Holy Scripture lies the source and ground of their preaching and authority. By the preaching of the word they seek to bring those who are not Christians into the fellowship of Christ. The Christian message needs also to be unfolded to the faithful, in order to deepen their knowledge of God and their response of grateful faith. But a true faith calls for beliefs that are correct and lives that endorse the Gospel. So the ministers have to guide the community and to advise individuals with regard to the implications of commitment to Christ. Because God's concern is not only for the welfare of the Church but also for the whole of creation, they must also lead their communities in the service of humanity. Church and people have continually to be brought under the guidance of the apostolic faith. In all these ways a ministerial vocation implies a responsibility for the word of God supported by constant prayer (cf. Acts 6.4).

11   The part of the ministers in the celebration of the sacraments is one with their responsibility for ministry of the word. In both word and sacrament Christians meet the living Word of God. The responsibility of the ministers in the Christian community involves them in being not only the persons who normally administer baptism, but also those who admit converts to the communion of the faithful and restore those who have fallen away. Authority to pronounce God's forgiveness of sin, given to bishops and presbyters at their ordination, is exercised by them to

bring Christians to a closer communion with God and with their fellow men through Christ and to assure them of God's continuing love and mercy.

12   To proclaim reconciliation in Christ and to manifest his reconciling love belong to the continuing mission of the Church. The central act of worship, the eucharist, is the memorial of that reconciliation and nourishes the Church's life for the fulfilment of its mission. Hence it is right that he who has oversight in the church and is the focus of its unity should preside at the celebration of the eucharist. Evidence as early as Ignatius shows that, at least in some churches, the man exercising this oversight presided at the eucharist and no other could do so without his consent (*Letter to the Smyrnaeans*, 8.1).

13   The priestly sacrifice of Jesus was unique, as is also his continuing High Priesthood. Despite the fact that in the New Testament ministers are never called 'priests' (*hiereis*),[2] Christians came to see the priestly role of Christ reflected in these ministers and used priestly terms in describing them. Because the eucharist is the memorial of the sacrifice of Christ, the action of the presiding minister in reciting again the words of Christ at the last supper and distributing to the assembly the holy gifts is seen to stand in a sacramental relation to what Christ himself did in offering his own sacrifice. So our two traditions commonly use priestly terms in speaking about the ordained ministry. Such language does not imply any negation of the once-for-all sacrifice of Christ by any addition or repetition. There is in the eucharist a memorial (*anamnesis*)[3] of the totality of God's reconciling action in

[2] In the English language the word 'priest' is used to translate two distinct Greek words, *hiereus* which belongs to the cultic order and *presbyteros* which designates an elder in the community.

[3] Cf. Eucharist, para. 5.

Christ, who through his minister presides at the Lord's Supper and gives himself sacramentally. So it is because the eucharist is central in the Church's life that the essential nature of the Christian ministry, however this may be expressed, is most clearly seen in its celebration; for, in the eucharist, thanksgiving is offered to God, the gospel of salvation is proclaimed in word and sacrament, and the community is knit together as one body in Christ. Christian ministers are members of this redeemed community. Not only do they share through baptism in the priesthood of the people of God, but they are— particularly in presiding at the eucharist—representative of the whole Church in the fulfilment of its priestly vocation of self-offering to God as a living sacrifice (Rom. 12.1). Nevertheless their ministry is not an extension of the common Christian priesthood but belongs to another realm of the gifts of the Spirit. It exists to help the Church to be 'a royal priesthood, a holy nation, God's own people, to declare the wonderful deeds of him who called [them] out of darkness into his marvellous light' (1 Pet. 2.9).

II *Vocation and Ordination*

14 Ordination denotes entry into this apostolic and God-given ministry, which serves and signifies the unity of the local churches in themselves and with one another. Every individual act of ordination is therefore an expression of the continuing apostolicity and catholicity of the whole Church. Just as the original apostles did not choose themselves but were chosen and commissioned by Jesus, so those who are ordained are called by Christ in the Church and through the Church. Not only is their vocation from Christ but their qualification for exercising such a ministry is the gift of the Spirit: 'our sufficiency is

from God, who has qualified us to be ministers of a new covenant, not in a written code but in the Spirit' (2 Cor. 3.5—6). This is expressed in ordination, when the bishop prays God to grant the gift of the Holy Spirit and lays hands on the candidate as the outward sign of the gifts bestowed. Because ministry is in and for the community and because ordination is an act in which the whole Church of God is involved, this prayer and laying on of hands take place within the context of the eucharist.

15   In this sacramental act,[4] the gift of God is bestowed upon the ministers, with the promise of divine grace for their work and for their sanctification; the ministry of Christ is presented to them as a model for their own; and the Spirit seals those whom he has chosen and consecrated. Just as Christ has united the Church inseparably with himself, and as God calls all the faithful to lifelong discipleship, so the gifts and calling of God to the ministers are irrevocable. For this reason, ordination is unrepeatable in both our churches.

16   Both presbyters and deacons are ordained by the bishop. In the ordination of a presbyter the presbyters present join the bishop in the laying on of hands, thus signifying the shared nature of the commission entrusted to them. In the ordination of a new bishop, other bishops lay hands on him, as they request the gift of the Spirit for his ministry and receive him into their ministerial fellowship. Because they are entrusted with the oversight of other churches, this participation in his ordination signifies that this new bishop and his church are within the communion

---

[4] Anglican use of the word 'sacrament' with reference to ordination is limited by the distinction drawn in the Thirty-nine Articles (Article 25) between the two 'sacraments of the Gospel' and the 'five commonly called sacraments'. Article 25 does not deny these latter the name 'sacrament', but differentiates between them and the 'two sacraments ordained by Christ' described in the Catechism as 'necessary to salvation' for all men.

of churches. Moreover, because they are representative of
their churches in fidelity to the teaching and mission of the
apostles and are members of the episcopal college, their
participation also ensures the historical continuity of this
church with the apostolic Church and of its bishop with
the original apostolic ministry. The communion of the
churches in mission , faith, and holiness, through time and
space, is thus symbolized and maintained in the bishop.
Here are comprised the essential features of what is meant
in our two traditions by ordination in the apostolic
succession.

Conclusion

17 We are fully aware of the issues raised by the
judgement of the Roman Catholic Church on Anglican
Orders. The development of the thinking in our two
communions regarding the nature of the Church and of
the ordained ministry, as represented in our Statement,
has, we consider, put these issues in a new context.
Agreement on the nature of ministry is prior to the
consideration of the mutual recognition of ministries.
What we have to say represents the consensus of the
Commission on essential matters where it considers that
doctrine admits no divergence. It will be clear that we
have not yet broached the wide-ranging problems of
authority which may arise in any discussion of ministry,
nor the question of primacy. We are aware that present
understanding of such matters remains an obstacle to the
reconciliation of our churches in the one Communion we
desire, and the Commission is now turning to the
examination of the issues involved. Nevertheless we
consider that our consensus, on questions where

agreement is indispensable for unity, offers a positive contribution to the reconciliation of our churches and of their ministries.

Elucidation (1979)

Comments and Criticisms

1   After the publication of the Statement *Ministry and Ordination*, the Commission received comments and criticisms, among which it judged the following to be of special concern.

It has been suggested that in the discussion of ministry insufficient attention was given to the priesthood of the whole people of God, so that the document seemed to have too clerical an emphasis. In this connection it has also been said that the distinction between this priesthood of all the faithful and the priesthood of the ordained ministry was not clearly enough explained. Questions have also been raised about the Commission's treatment of the origins and historical development of the ordained ministry and its threefold form; about its comparison of that development with the emergence of the canon of Scripture; and about its views on the place of episcopacy within *episcope* as it is outlined in the Statement (para. 9).

Some have wondered whether the Statement adequately expressed the sacramental nature of the rite of ordination, others whether this aspect has been over-emphasized. The Commission has been asked to consider the implications of the Statement for the question of the ordination of women. There have also been inquiries about the bearing of the Statement upon the problem of recognizing the validity of Anglican Orders.

Priesthood

2   In common Christian usage the term *priesthood* is employed in three distinct ways: the priesthood of Christ, the priesthood of the people of God, the priesthood of the ordained ministry.

The priesthood of Christ is unique. He is our High Priest who has reconciled mankind with the Father. All other priesthood derives from his and is wholly dependent upon it.

The priesthood of the whole people of God (1 Peter 2.5) is the consequence of incorporation by baptism into Christ. This priesthood of all the faithful (para. 7) is not a matter of disagreement between us. In a document primarily concerned with the ordained ministry, the Commission did not consider it necessary to develop the subject further than it has already done in the Statement. Here the ordained ministry is firmly placed in the context of the ministry of the whole Church and exists for the service of all the faithful.

The Statement (para. 13) explains that the ordained ministry is called priestly principally because it has a particular sacramental relationship with Christ as High Priest. At the eucharist Christ's people do what he commanded in memory of himself and Christ unites them sacramentally with himself in his self-offering. But in this action it is only the ordained minister who presides at the eucharist, in which, in the name of Christ and on behalf of his Church, he recites the narrative of the institution of the Last Supper, and invokes the Holy Spirit upon the gifts.

The word *priesthood* is used by way of analogy when it is applied to the people of God and to the ordained ministry. These are two distinct realities which relate, each in its own way, to the high priesthood of Christ, the unique priesthood of the new covenant, which is their source and model. These considerations should be borne in mind throughout para. 13, and in particular they indicate the significance of the statement that the ordained ministry 'is not an extension of the common Christian priesthood but belongs to another realm of the gifts of the Spirit'.

In this as in other cases the early Church found it

41

necessary for its understanding and exposition of the faith to employ terminology in ways in which it was not used in the New Testament. Today in seeking to give an account of our faith both our communions, in the interpretation of the Scriptures, take cognisance of the Church's growing understanding of Christian truth (cf. Authority I, paras. 2, 3, and 15).

Sacramentality of Ordination

3   The phrase 'in this sacramental act' in para. 15 has caused anxiety on two different counts: that this phrase seems to give the sacrament of ordination the same status as the two 'sacraments of the Gospel'; and that it does not adequately express the full sacramentality of ordination.

Both traditions agree that a sacramental rite is a visible sign through which the grace of God is given by the Holy Spirit in the Church. The rite of ordination is one of these sacramental rites. Those who are ordained by prayer and the laying on of hands receive their ministry from Christ through those designated in the Church to hand it on; together with the office they are given the grace needed for its fulfilment (cf. para. 14). Since New Testament times the Church has required such recognition and authorization for those who are to exercise the principal functions of *episcope* in the name of Christ. This is what both traditions mean by the sacramental rite of ordination.

Both traditions affirm the pre-eminence of baptism and the eucharist as sacraments 'necessary to salvation'. This does not diminish their understanding of the sacramental nature of ordination, as to which there is no significant disagreement between them.

Origins and Development of the Ordained Ministry

4   Our treatment of the origins of the ordained ministry has been criticized. While the evidence leaves ground for

differences of interpretation, it is enough for our purpose to recall that, from the beginning of the Christian Church, there existed *episcope* in the community, however its various responsibilities were distributed and described, and whatever the names given to those who exercise it (cf. paras. 8, 9, and especially 6). It is generally agreed that, within the first century, evidence of ordination such as we have described above is provided by the *First Epistle of Clement*, chapters 40—44, commonly dated 95 A.D. Some New Testament passages appear to imply the same conclusion, e.g. Acts 14.23. Early in the second century, the pattern of a threefold ministry centred on episcopacy was already discernible, and probably widely found (cf. the Epistles of Ignatius to the *Ephesians*, 4; *Magnesians*, 13; *Trallians*, 2; *Philadelphians*, 2; *Smyrnaeans*, 8). It was recognized that such ministry must be in continuity not only with the apostolic faith but also with the commission given to the apostles (cf. the *First Epistle of Clement*, 42).

Our intention in drawing a parallel between this emergence of the threefold ministry and the formation of the New Testament canon was to point to comparable processes of gradual development without determining whether the comparison could be carried further (cf. para. 6). The threefold ministry remained universal until the divisions of Western Christianity in the sixteenth century. However, both our communions have retained it.

We both maintain that *episcope* must be exercised by ministers ordained in the apostolic succession (cf. para. 16). Both our communions have retained and remained faithful to the threefold ministry centred on episcopacy as the form in which this *episcope* is to be exercised. Because our task was limited to examining relations between our two communions, we did not enter into the question whether there is any other form in which this *episcope* can be realized.

Ordination of Women

5   Since the publication of the Statement there have been rapid developments with regard to the ordination of women. In those churches of the Anglican Communion where canonical ordinations of women have taken place, the bishops concerned believe that their action implies no departure from the traditional doctrine of the ordained ministry (as expounded, for instance, in the Statement). While the Commission realizes that the ordination of women has created for the Roman Catholic Church a new and grave obstacle to the reconciliation of our communions (cf. Letter of Pope Paul VI to Archbishop Donald Coggan, 23 March 1976, AAS 68), it believes that the principles upon which its doctrinal agreement rests are not affected by such ordinations; for it was concerned with the origin and nature of the ordained ministry and not with the question who can or cannot be ordained. Objections, however substantial, to the ordination of women are of a different kind from objections raised in the past against the validity of Anglican Orders in general.

Anglican Orders

6   In answer to the questions concerning the significance of the Agreed Statements for the mutual recognition of ministry, the Commission has affirmed that a consensus has been reached that places the questions in a new context (cf. para. 17). It believes that our agreement on the essentials of eucharistic faith with regard to the sacramental presence of Christ and the sacrificial dimension of the eucharist, and on the nature and purpose of priesthood, ordination, and apostolic succession, is the new context in which the questions should now be

discussed. This calls for a reappraisal of the verdict on Anglican Orders in *Apostolicae Curae* (1896).

Mutual recognition presupposes acceptance of the apostolicity of each other's ministry. The Commission believes that its agreements have demonstrated a consensus in faith on eucharist and ministry which has brought closer the possibility of such acceptance. It hopes that its own conviction will be shared by members of both our communions; but mutual recognition can only be achieved by the decision of our authorities. It has been our mandate to offer to them the basis upon which they may make this decision.

Authority in the Church   I

Co-Chairmen's Preface

The Malta Report of the Anglican—Roman Catholic Joint Preparatory Commission (1968) outlined the large measure of agreement in faith which exists between the Roman Catholic Church and the churches of the Anglican Communion (para. 7). It then went on to note three specific areas of doctrinal disagreement. These were listed in the Report as matters for joint investigation. Accordingly the Anglican—Roman Catholic International Commission, proposed by the Report, was recommended to examine jointly 'the question of intercommunion, and the related matters of Church and Ministry', and 'the question of authority, its nature, exercise, and implications'.

To our previous Agreed Statements on the Eucharist (Windsor 1971) and Ministry (Canterbury 1973) we now add an Agreed Statement on Authority in the Church (Venice 1976). The Commission thus submits its work to the authorities who appointed it and, with their permission, offers it to our churches.

The question of authority in the Church has long been recognized as crucial to the growth in unity of the Roman Catholic Church and the churches of the Anglican Communion. It was precisely in the problem of papal primacy that our historical divisions found their unhappy origin. Hence, however significant our consensus on the doctrine of the eucharist and of the ministry, unresolved questions on the nature and exercise of authority in the Church would hinder the growing experience of unity which is the pattern of our present relations.

The present Statement has, we believe, made a significant contribution to the resolution of these questions. Our consensus covers a very wide area; though we have not been able to resolve some of the difficulties of

49

Anglicans concerning Roman Catholic belief relating to the office of the bishop of Rome, we hope and trust that our analysis has placed these problems in a proper perspective.

There is much in the document, as in our other documents, which presents the ideal of the Church as willed by Christ. History shows how the Church has often failed to achieve this ideal. An awareness of this distinction between the ideal and the actual is important both for the reading of the document and for the understanding of the method we have pursued.

The consensus we have reached, if it is to be accepted by our two communities, would have, we insist, important consequences. Common recognition of Roman primacy would bring changes not only to the Anglican Communion but also to the Roman Catholic Church. On both sides the readiness to learn, necessary to the achievement of such a wider *koinonia*, would demand humility and charity. The prospect should be met with faith, not fear. Communion with the see of Rome would bring to the churches of the Anglican Communion not only a wider *koinonia* but also a strengthening of the power to realize its traditional ideal of diversity in unity. Roman Catholics, on their side, would be enriched by the presence of a particular tradition of spirituality and scholarship, the lack of which has deprived the Roman Catholic Church of a precious element in the Christian heritage. The Roman Catholic Church has much to learn from the Anglican synodical tradition of involving the laity in the life and mission of the Church. We are convinced, therefore, that our degree of agreement, which argues for greater communion between our churches, can make a profound contribution to the witness of Christianity in our contemporary society.

It is in this light that we would wish to submit our

conclusions to our respective authorities, believing that our work, indebted, as it is, to many sources outside the Commission as well as to its own labours, will be of service not only to ourselves but to Christians of other traditions in our common quest for the unity of Christ's Church.

September 1976   H. R. McADOO
                                                    ALAN C. CLARK

The Statement (1976)

Introduction

1 The confession of Christ as Lord is the heart of the Christian faith. To him God has given all authority in heaven and on earth. As Lord of the Church he bestows the Holy Spirit to create a communion of men with God and with one another. To bring this *koinonia* to perfection is God's eternal purpose. The Church exists to serve the fulfilment of this purpose when God will be all in all.

I *Christian Authority*

2 Through the gift of the Spirit the apostolic community came to recognize in the words and deeds of Jesus the saving activity of God and their mission to proclaim to all men the good news of salvation. Therefore they preached Jesus through whom God has spoken finally to men. Assisted by the Holy Spirit they transmitted what they had heard and seen of the life and words of Jesus and their interpretation of his redemptive work. Consequently the inspired documents in which this is related came to be accepted by the Church as a normative record of the authentic foundation of the faith. To these the Church has recourse for the inspiration of its life and mission; to these the Church refers its teaching and practice. Through these written words the authority of the Word of God is conveyed. Entrusted with these documents, the Christian community is enabled by the Holy Spirit to live out the Gospel and so to be led into all truth. It is therefore given the capacity to assess its faith and life and to speak to the world in the name of Christ. Shared commitment and belief create a common mind in determining how the Gospel should be interpreted and obeyed. By reference to this common faith each person tests the truth of his own belief.

3   The Spirit of the risen Lord, who indwells the Christian community, continues to maintain the people of God in obedience to the Father's will. He safeguards their faithfulness to the revelation of Jesus Christ and equips them for their mission in the world. By this action of the Holy Spirit the authority of the Lord is active in the Church. Through incorporation into Christ and obedience to him Christians are made open to one another and assume mutual obligations. Since the Lordship of Christ is universal, the community also bears a responsibility towards all mankind, which demands participation in all that promotes the good of society and responsiveness to every form of human need. The common life in the body of Christ equips the community and each of its members with what they need to fulfil this responsibility: they are enabled so to live that the authority of Christ will be mediated through them. This is Christian authority: when Christians so act and speak, men perceive the authoritative word of Christ.

II   *Authority in the Church*

4   The Church is a community which consciously seeks to submit to Jesus Christ. By sharing in the life of the Spirit all find within the *koinonia* the means to be faithful to the revelation of their Lord. Some respond more fully to his call; by the inner quality of their life they win a respect which allows them to speak in Christ's name with authority.

. 5   The Holy Spirit also gives to some individuals and communities special gifts for the benefit of the Church, which entitle them to speak and be heeded (e.g. Eph. 4.11, 12; 1 Cor. 12.4–11).

Among these gifts of the Spirit for the edification of the Church is the *episcope* of the ordained ministry. There are some whom the Holy Spirit commissions through ordination for service to the whole community. They exercise their authority in fulfilling ministerial functions related to 'the apostles' teaching and fellowship, to the breaking of bread and the prayers' (Acts 2.42). This pastoral authority belongs primarily to the bishop, who is responsible for preserving and promoting the integrity of the *koinonia* in order to further the Church's response to the Lordship of Christ and its commitment to mission. Since the bishop has general oversight of the community, he can require the compliance necessary to maintain faith and charity in its daily life. He does not, however, act alone. All those who have ministerial authority must recognize their mutual responsibility and interdependence. This service of the Church, officially entrusted only to ordained ministers, is intrinsic to the Church's structure according to the mandate given by Christ and recognized by the community. This is yet another form of authority.

6   The perception of God's will for his Church does not belong only to the ordained ministry but is shared by all its members. All who live faithfully within the *koinonia* may become sensitive to the leading of the Spirit and be brought towards a deeper understanding of the Gospel and of its implications in diverse cultures and changing situations. Ordained ministers commissioned to discern these insights and give authoritative expression to them, are part of the community, sharing its quest for understanding the Gospel in obedience to Christ and receptive to the needs and concerns of all.

The community, for its part, must respond to and assess the insights and teaching of the ordained ministers. Through this continuing process of discernment and response, in which the faith is expressed and the Gospel is pastorally applied, the Holy Spirit declares the authority of the Lord Jesus Christ, and the faithful may live freely under the discipline of the Gospel.

7   It is by such means as these that the Holy Spirit keeps
the Church under the Lordship of Christ, who, taking full
account of human weakness, has promised never to abandon
his people. The authorities in the Church cannot adequately
reflect Christ's authority because they are still subject to the
limitations and sinfulness of human nature. Awareness of
this inadequacy is a continual summons to reform.

III   *Authority in the Communion of the Churches*

8   The *koinonia* is realized not only in the local Christian
communities, but also in the communion of these communities with one another. The unity of local communities
under one bishop constitutes what is commonly meant in
our two communions by 'a local church', though the
expression is sometimes used in other ways. Each local
church is rooted in the witness of the apostles and
entrusted with the apostolic mission. Faithful to the
Gospel, celebrating the one eucharist and dedicated to the
service of the same Lord, it is the Church of Christ. In spite
of diversities each local church recognizes its own essential
features in the others and its true identity with them. The
authoritative action and proclamation of the people of
God to the world therefore are not simply the
responsibilities of each church acting separately, but of all
the local churches together. The spiritual gifts of one may
be an inspiration to the others. Since each bishop must
ensure that the local community is distinctively Christian
he has to make it aware of the universal communion of
which it is part. The bishop expresses this unity of his
church with the others: this is symbolized by the participation of several bishops in his ordination.

9   Ever since the Council of Jerusalem (Acts 15) the

churches have realized the need to express and strengthen the *koinonia* by coming together to discuss matters of mutual concern and to meet contemporary challenges. Such gatherings may be either regional or world-wide. Through such meetings the Church, determined to be obedient to Christ and faithful to its vocation, formulates its rule of faith and orders its life. In all these councils, whether of bishops only, or of bishops, clergy, and laity, decisions are authoritative when they express the common faith and mind of the Church. The decisions of what has traditionally been called an 'ecumenical council' are binding upon the whole Church; those of a regional council or synod bind only the churches it represents. Such decrees are to be received by the local churches as expressing the mind of the Church. This exercise of authority, far from being an imposition, is designed to strengthen the life and mission of the local churches and of their members.

10   Early in the history of the Church a function of oversight of the other bishops of their regions was assigned to bishops of prominent sees. Concern to keep the churches faithful to the will of Christ was among the considerations which contributed to this development. This practice has continued to the present day. This form of *episcope* is a service to the Church carried out in co-responsibility with all the bishops of the region; for every bishop receives at ordination both responsibility for his local church and the obligation to maintain it in living awareness and practical service of the other churches. The Church of God is found in each of them and in their *koinonia*.

11   The purpose of *koinonia* is the realization of the will of Christ: 'Father, keep them in thy name, which thou hast given me, that they may be one, even as we are one. . . .

so that the world may believe that thou hast sent me'
(John 17.11, 21). The bishop of a principal see should seek
the fulfilment of this will of Christ in the churches of his
region. It is his duty to assist the bishops to promote in
their churches right teaching, holiness of life, brotherly
unity, and the Church's mission to the world. When he
perceives a serious deficiency in the life or mission of one of
the churches he is bound, if necessary, to call the local
bishop's attention to it and to offer assistance. There will
also be occasions when he has to assist other bishops to
reach a common mind with regard to their shared needs
and difficulties. Sharing together and active mutual
concern are indispensable to the churches' effective
witness to Christ.

12   It is within the context of this historical development
that the see of Rome, whose prominence was associated
with the death there of Peter and Paul, eventually became
the principal centre in matters concerning the Church
universal.

The importance of the bishop of Rome among his
brother bishops, as explained by analogy with the position
of Peter among the apostles, was interpreted as Christ's
will for his Church.

On the basis of this analogy the First Vatican Council
affirmed that this service was necessary to the unity of the
whole Church. Far from overriding the authority of the
bishops in their own dioceses, this service was explicitly
intended to support them in their ministry of oversight.
The Second Vatican Council placed this service in the
wider context of the shared responsibility of all the
bishops. The teaching of these councils shows that
communion with the bishop of Rome does not imply
submission to an authority which would stifle the
distinctive features of the local churches. The purpose of

this episcopal function of the bishop of Rome is to promote Christian fellowship in faithfulness to the teaching of the apostles.

The theological interpretation of this primacy and the administrative structures through which it has been exercised have varied considerably through the centuries. Neither theory nor practice, however, has ever fully reflected these ideals. Sometimes functions assumed by the see of Rome were not necessarily linked to the primacy: sometimes the conduct of the occupant of this see has been unworthy of his office: sometimes the image of this office has been obscured by interpretations placed upon it: and sometimes external pressures have made its proper exercise almost impossible. Yet the primacy, rightly understood, implies that the bishop of Rome exercises his oversight in order to guard and promote the faithfulness of all the churches to Christ and one another. Communion with him is intended as a safeguard of the catholicity of each local church, and as a sign of the communion of all the churches.

IV *Authority in Matters of Faith*

13   A local church cannot be truly faithful to Christ if it does not desire to foster universal communion, the embodiment of that unity for which Christ prayed. This communion is founded on faith in Jesus Christ, the incarnate Son of God, crucified, risen, ascended, and now living through his Spirit in the Church. Every local church must therefore ever seek a deeper understanding and clearer expression of this common faith, both of which are threatened when churches are isolated by division.

14   The Church's purpose in its proclamation is to lead mankind to accept God's saving work in Christ, an acceptance which not only requires intellectual assent but

also demands the response of the whole person. In order to clarify and transmit what is believed and to build up and safeguard the Christian life, the Church has found the formulation of creeds, conciliar definitions, and other statements of belief indispensable. But these are always instrumental to the truth which they are intended to convey.

15 The Church's life and work are shaped by its historical origins, by its subsequent experience, and by its endeavour to make the relevance of the Gospel plain to every generation. Through reflection upon the word, through the proclamation of the Gospel, through baptism, through worship, especially the eucharist, the people of God are moved to the living remembrance of Jesus Christ and of the experience and witness of the apostolic community. This remembrance supports and guides them in their search for language which will effectively communicate the meaning of the Gospel.

All generations and cultures must be helped to understand that the good news of salvation is also for them. It is not enough for the Church simply to repeat the original apostolic words. It has also prophetically to translate them in order that the hearers in their situation may understand and respond to them. All such restatement must be consonant with the apostolic witness recorded in the Scriptures; for in this witness the preaching and teaching of ministers, and statements of local and universal councils, have to find their ground and consistency. Although these clarifications are conditioned by the circumstances which prompted them, some of their perceptions may be of lasting value. In this process the Church itself may come to see more clearly the implications of the Gospel. This is why the Church has endorsed certain formulas as authentic expressions of its witness, whose significance transcends the setting in which they were first formulated. This is not to claim that these formulas are the only possible, or even the most exact, way of expressing the faith, or that they can never be improved. Even when a doctrinal definition is regarded by the Christian community as part of its permanent teaching, this does not exclude subsequent restatement. Although the categories of thought and the mode of expression may be superseded, restatement always builds upon, and does not contradict, the truth intended by the original definition.

16   Local councils held from the second century determined the limits of the New Testament, and gave to the Church a canon which has remained normative. The action of a council in making such a decision on so momentous a matter implies an assurance that the Lord himself is present when his people assemble in his name (Matt. 18.20), and that a council may say, 'it has seemed good to the Holy Spirit and to us' (Acts 15.28). The conciliar mode of authority exercised in the matter of the canon has also been applied to questions of discipline and of fundamental doctrine. When decisions (as at Nicaea in 325) affect the entire Church and deal with controverted matters which have been widely and seriously debated, it is important to establish criteria for the recognition and reception of conciliar definitions and disciplinary decisions. A substantial part in the process of reception is played by the subject matter of the definitions and by the response of the faithful. This process is often gradual, as the decisions come to be seen in perspective through the Spirit's continuing guidance of the whole Church.

17   Among the complex historical factors which contributed to the recognition of conciliar decisions considerable weight attached to their confirmation by the principal

sees, and in particular by the see of Rome. At an early period other local churches actively sought the support and approbation of the church in Rome; and in course of time the agreement of the Roman see was regarded as necessary to the general acceptance of synodal decisions in major matters of more than regional concern, and also, eventually, to their canonical validity. By their agreement or disagreement the local church of Rome and its bishop fulfilled their responsibility towards other local churches and their bishops for maintaining the whole Church in the truth. In addition the bishop of Rome was also led to intervene in controversies relating to matters of faith—in most cases in response to appeals made to him, but sometimes on his own initiative.

18   In its mission to proclaim and safeguard the Gospel the Church has the obligation and the competence to make declarations in matters of faith. This mission involves the whole people of God, among whom some may rediscover or perceive more clearly than others certain aspects of the saving truth. At times there result conflict and debate. Customs, accepted positions, beliefs, formulations, and practices, as well as innovations and re-interpretations, may be shown to be inadequate, mistaken, or even inconsistent with the Gospel. When conflict endangers unity or threatens to distort the Gospel the Church must have effective means for resolving it.

In both our traditions the appeal to Scripture, to the creeds, to the Fathers, and to the definitions of the councils of the early Church is regarded as basic and normative.[1] But the bishops have a special responsibility for promoting truth and discerning error, and the interaction of bishop and people in its exercise is a safeguard of Christian

---

[1] This is emphasized in the Anglican tradition. Cf. the Lambeth Conferences of 1948 and 1968.

life and fidelity. The teaching of the faith and the ordering of life in the Christian community require a daily exercise of this responsibility; but there is no guarantee that those who have an everyday responsibility will—any more than other members—invariably be free from errors of judgement, will never tolerate abuses, and will never distort the truth. Yet, in Christian hope, we are confident that such failures cannot destroy the Church's ability to proclaim the Gospel and to show forth the Christian life; for we believe that Christ will not desert his Church and that the Holy Spirit will lead it into all truth. That is why the Church, in spite of its failures, can be described as indefectible.

V *Conciliar and Primatial Authority*

19 In times of crisis or when fundamental matters of faith are in question, the Church can make judgements, consonant with Scripture, which are authoritative. When the Church meets in ecumenical council its decisions on fundamental matters of faith exclude what is erroneous. Through the Holy Spirit the Church commits itself to these judgements, recognizing that, being faithful to Scripture and consistent with Tradition, they are by the same Spirit protected from error. They do not add to the truth but, although not exhaustive, they clarify the Church's understanding of it. In discharging this responsibility bishops share in a special gift of Christ to his Church. Whatever further clarification or interpretation may be propounded by the Church, the truth expressed will always be confessed. This binding authority does not belong to every conciliar decree, but only to those which formulate the central truths of salvation. This authority is ascribed in both our traditions to decisions of the

ecumenical councils of the first centuries.[2]

20   The bishops are collectively responsible for defending and interpreting the apostolic faith. The primacy accorded to a bishop implies that, after consulting his fellow bishops, he may speak in their name and express their mind. The recognition of his position by the faithful creates an expectation that on occasion he will take an initiative in speaking for the Church. Primatial statements are only one way by which the Holy Spirit keeps the people of God faithful to the truth of the Gospel.

21   If primacy is to be a genuine expression of *episcope* it will foster the *koinonia* by helping the bishops in their task of apostolic leadership both in their local church and in the Church universal. Primacy fulfils its purpose by helping the churches to listen to one another, to grow in love and unity, and to strive together towards the fullness of Christian life and witness; it respects and promotes Christian freedom and spontaneity; it does not seek uniformity where diversity is legitimate, or centralize administration to the detriment of local churches.

A primate exercises his ministry not in isolation but in collegial association with his brother bishops. His intervention in the affairs of a local church should not be made in such a way as to usurp the responsibility of its bishop.

22   Although primacy and conciliarity are complementary elements of *episcope* it has often happened that one has been emphasized at the expense of the other, even to the point of serious imbalance. When churches have been separated from one another, this danger has

[2] Since our historical divisions, the Roman Catholic Church has continued the practice of holding general councils of its bishops, some of which it has designated as ecumenical. The churches of the Anglican Communion have developed other forms of conciliarity.

been increased. The *koinonia* of the churches requires that a proper balance be preserved between the two with the responsible participation of the whole people of God.

23   If God's will for the unity in love and truth of the whole Christian community is to be fulfilled, this general pattern of the complementary primatial and conciliar aspects of *episcope* serving the *koinonia* of the churches needs to be realized at the universal level. The only see which makes any claim to universal primacy and which has exercised and still exercises such *episcope* is the see of Rome, the city where Peter and Paul died.

It seems appropriate that in any future union a universal primacy such as has been described should be held by that see.

VI   *Problems and Prospects*

24   What we have written here amounts to a consensus on authority in the Church and, in particular, on the basic principles of primacy. This consensus is of fundamental importance. While it does not wholly resolve all the problems associated with papal primacy, it provides us with a solid basis for confronting them. It is when we move from these basic principles to particular claims of papal primacy and to its exercise that problems arise, the gravity of which will be variously judged:

(*a*) Claims on behalf of the Roman see as commonly presented in the past have put a greater weight on the Petrine texts (Matt. 16.18, 19; Luke 22.31, 32; John 21. 15–17) than they are generally thought to be able to bear. However, many Roman Catholic scholars do not now feel it necessary to stand by former exegesis of these texts in every respect.

(*b*) The First Vatican Council of 1870 uses the language of 'divine right' of the successors of Peter. This language has no clear interpretation in modern Roman Catholic theology. If it is understood as affirming that the universal primacy of the bishop of Rome is part of God's design for the universal *koinonia* then it need not be a matter of disagreement. But if it were further implied that as long as a church is not in communion with the bishop of Rome, it is regarded by the Roman Catholic Church as less than fully a church, a difficulty would remain: for some this difficulty would be removed by simply restoring communion, but to others the implication would itself be an obstacle to entering into communion with Rome.

(*c*) Anglicans find grave difficulty in the affirmation that the pope can be infallible in his teaching. It must, however, be borne in mind that the doctrine of infallibility[3] is hedged round by very rigorous conditions laid down at the First Vatican Council. These conditions preclude the idea that the pope is an inspired oracle communicating fresh revelation, or that he can speak independently of his fellow bishops and the Church, or on matters not concerning faith or morals. For the Roman Catholic Church the pope's dogmatic definitions, which, fulfilling the criteria of infallibility, are preserved from error, do no more but no less than express the mind of the Church on issues concerning the divine revelation. Even so, special difficulties are created by the recent Marian dogmas, because Anglicans doubt the appropriateness, or even the possibility, of defining them as essential to the faith of believers.

(*d*) The claim that the pope possesses universal immediate jurisdiction, the limits of which are not clearly specified, is a source of anxiety to Anglicans who fear that the way is thus open to its illegitimate or uncontrolled use.

---

[3] 'Infallibility' is a technical term which does not bear precisely the same meaning as the word does in common usage. Its theological sense is seen in paras. 15 and 19 above.

Nevertheless, the First Vatican Council intended that the papal primacy should be exercised only to maintain and never to erode the structures of the local churches. The Roman Catholic Church is today seeking to replace the juridical outlook of the nineteenth century by a more pastoral understanding of authority in the Church.

25   In spite of the difficulties just mentioned, we believe that this Statement on Authority in the Church represents a significant convergence with far-reaching consequences. For a considerable period theologians in our two traditions, without compromising their respective allegiances, have worked on common problems with the same methods. In the process they have come to see old problems in new horizons and have experienced a theological convergence which has often taken them by surprise.

In our three Agreed Statements we have endeavoured to get behind the opposed and entrenched positions of past controversies. We have tried to reassess what are the real issues to be resolved. We have often deliberately avoided the vocabulary of past polemics, not with any intention of evading the real difficulties that provoked them, but because the emotive associations of such language have often obscured the truth. For the future relations between our churches the doctrinal convergence which we have experienced offers hope that remaining difficulties can be resolved.

Conclusion

26   The Malta Report of 1968 envisaged the coming together of the Roman Catholic Church and the churches of the Anglican Communion in terms of 'unity by stages'. We have reached agreements on the doctrines of the eucharist, ministry, and, apart from the qualifications of para. 24, authority. Doctrinal agreements reached by

theological commissions cannot, however, by themselves achieve the goal of Christian unity. Accordingly, we submit our Statements to our respective authorities to consider whether or not they are judged to express on these central subjects a unity at the level of faith which not only justifies but requires action to bring about a closer sharing between our two communions in life, worship, and mission.

Elucidation (1981)

Comments and Criticisms

1 After the publication of the first Statement on Authority the Commission received comments and criticisms. Some of the questions raised, such as the request for a clarification of the relation between infallibility and indefectibility, find an answer in the second Statement on Authority. Another question, concerning our understanding of *koinonia*, is answered in the Introduction to this Final Report, where we show how the concept underlies all our Statements.

Behind many reactions to the Statement is a degree of uneasiness as to whether sufficient attention is paid to the primary authority of Scripture, with the result that certain developments are given an authority comparable to that of Scripture. Serious questions have also been asked about councils and reception, and some commentators have claimed that what the Statement says about the protection of an ecumenical council from error is in conflict with Article 21 of the Anglican Articles of Religion. It has been suggested that the treatment of the place and authority of the laity in the Church is inadequate. There have also been requests for a clarification of the nature of ministerial authority and of jurisdiction. Some questions have been asked about the status of regional primacies—for example, the patriarchal office as exercised in the Eastern churches. Finally, a recurring question has been whether the Commission is suggesting that a universal primacy is a theological necessity simply because one has existed or been claimed.

In what follows the Commission attempts to address itself to these problems and to elucidate the Statement as it bears on each of them. In seeking to answer the criticisms that have been received we have sometimes thought it necessary to go further and to elucidate the basic issues that underlie them. In all that we say we take for granted two fundamental principles—that Christian faith depends on divine revelation and that the Holy Spirit guides the Church in the understanding and transmission of revealed truth.

The Place of Scripture

2   Our documents have been criticized for failing to give an adequate account of the primary authority of Scripture in the Church, thereby making it possible for us to treat certain developments as possessing an authority comparable to that of Scripture itself. Our description of 'the inspired documents . . . as a normative record of the authentic foundation of the faith' (para. 2) has been felt to be an inadequate statement of the truth.

The basis of our approach to Scripture is the affirmation that Christ is God's final word to man—his eternal Word made flesh. He is the culmination of the diverse ways in which God has spoken since the beginning (Heb. 1. 1—3). In him God's saving and revealing purpose is fully and definitively realized.

The patriarchs and the prophets received and spoke the word of God in the Spirit. By the power of the same Spirit the Word of God became flesh and accomplished his ministry. At Pentecost the same Spirit was given to the disciples to enable them to recall and interpret what Jesus did and taught, and so to proclaim the Gospel in truth and power.

The person and work of Jesus Christ, preached by the apostles and set forth and interpreted in the New Testament writings, through the inspiration of the Holy Spirit, are the primary norm for Christian faith and life.

Jesus, as the Word of God, sums up in himself the whole of God's self-disclosure. The Church's essential task, therefore, in the exercise of its teaching office, is to unfold the full extent and implications of the mystery of Christ, under the guidance of the Spirit of the risen Lord.

No endeavour of the Church to express the truth can add to the revelation already given. Moreover, since the Scriptures are the uniquely inspired witness to divine revelation, the Church's expression of that revelation must be tested by its consonance with Scripture. This does not mean simply repeating the words of Scripture, but also both delving into their deeper significance and unravelling their implications for Christian belief and practice. It is impossible to do this without resorting to current language and thought. Consequently the teaching of the Church will often be expressed in words that are different from the original text of Scripture without being alien to its meaning. For instance, at the First Ecumenical Council the Church felt constrained to speak of the Son of God as 'of one substance with the Father' in order to expound the mystery of Christ. What was understood by the term 'of one substance' at this time was believed to express the content of Christian faith concerning Christ, even though the actual term is never used in the apostolic writings. This combination of permanence in the revealed truth and continuous exploration of its meaning is what is meant by Christian tradition. Some of the results of this reflection, which bear upon essential matters of faith, have come to be recognized as the authentic expression of Christian doctrine and therefore part of the 'deposit of faith'.

Tradition has been viewed in different ways. One approach is primarily concerned never to go beyond the bounds of Scripture. Under the guidance of the Spirit undiscovered riches and truths are sought in the Scriptures in order to illuminate the faith according to the needs of each generation. This is not slavery to the text of Scripture. It is an unfolding of the riches of the original revelation. Another approach, while different, does not necessarily contradict the former. In the conviction that the Holy Spirit is seeking to guide the Church into the fullness of truth, it draws upon everything in human experience and thought which will give to the content of the revelation its fullest expression and widest application. It is primarily concerned with the growth of the seed of God's word from age to age. This does not imply any denial of the uniqueness of the revelation. Because these two attitudes contain differing emphases, conflict may arise, even though in both cases the Church is seeking the fullness of revelation. The seal upon the truthfulness of the conclusions that result from this search will be the reception by the whole Church, since neither approach is immune from the possibility of error.

Councils and Reception

3   The Commission has been said to contradict Article 21 of the Articles of Religion in its affirmation that the decisions of what have traditionally been called ecumenical councils 'exclude what is erroneous'. The Commission is very far from implying that general councils cannot err and is well aware that they 'sometimes have erred'; for example the Councils of Ariminum and of Seleucia of 359 AD. Article 21 in fact affirms that general councils have authority only when their judgements 'may be declared that they be taken out of Holy Scripture'. According to the argument of the Statement also, only those judgements of general councils are guaranteed to 'exclude what is erroneous' or are 'protected from error' which have as their content 'fundamental matters of faith', which 'formulate the central truths of salvation' and

which are 'faithful to Scripture and consistent with Tradition'. 'They do not add to the truth but, although not exhaustive, they clarify the Church's understanding of it' (para. 19).

The Commission has also been asked to say whether reception by the whole people of God is part of the process which gives authority to the decisions of ecumenical councils.

By 'reception' we mean the fact that the people of God acknowledge such a decision or statement because they recognize in it the apostolic faith. They accept it because they discern a harmony between what is proposed to them and the *sensus fidelium* of the whole Church. As an example, the creed which we call Nicene has been received by the Church because in it the Church has recognized the apostolic faith. Reception does not create truth nor legitimize the decision: it is the final indication that such a decision has fulfilled the necessary conditions for it to be a true expression of the faith. In this acceptance the whole Church is involved in a continuous process of discernment and response (cf. para. 6).

The Commission therefore avoids two extreme positions. On the one hand it rejects the view that a definition has no authority until it is accepted by the whole Church or even derives its authority solely from that acceptance. Equally, the Commission denies that a council is so evidently self-sufficient that its definitions owe nothing to reception.

The Place of the Laity

4   The Commission has been accused of an over-emphasis upon the ordained ministry to the neglect of the laity.

In guarding and developing communion, every member has a part to play. Baptism gives everyone in the Church the right, and consequently the ability, to carry out his particular function in the body. The recognition of this fundamental right is of great importance. In different ways, even if sometimes hesitantly, our two Churches have sought to integrate in decision-making those who are not ordained.

The reason why the Statement spoke at length about the structure and the exercise of the authority of the ordained ministry was that this was the area where most difficulties appeared to exist. There was no devaluing of the proper and active role of the laity. For instance, we said that the Holy Spirit gives to some individuals and communities special gifts for the benefit of the Church (para. 5), that all the members of the Church share in the discovery of God's will (para. 6), that the *sensus fidelium* is a vital element in the comprehension of God's truth (para. 18), and that all bear witness to God's compassion for mankind and his concern for justice in the world (Ministry, para. 7).

The Authority of the Ordained Ministry

5 We have been asked to clarify the meaning of what some of our critics call 'hierarchical authority'—an expression we did not use. Here we are dealing with a form of authority which is inherent in the visible structure of the Church. By this we mean the authority attached to those ordained to exercise *episcope* in the Church. The Holy Spirit gives to each person power to fulfil his particular function within the body of Christ. Accordingly, those exercising *episcope* receive the grace appropriate to their calling and those for whom it is exercised must recognize and accept their God-given authority.

Both Anglicans and Roman Catholics, however, have criticized the emphasis we placed on a bishop's authority in certain circumstances to require compliance.

The specific oversight of the ordained ministry is exercised and acknowledged when a minister preaches the Gospel, presides at the eucharist, and seeks as pastor to lead the community truly to discern God's word and its relevance to their lives. When this responsibility laid upon a bishop (or other ordained minister under the direction of a bishop) requires him to declare a person to be in error in respect of doctrine or conduct, even to the point of exclusion from eucharistic communion, he is acting for the sake of the integrity of the community's faith and life. Both our communions have always recognized this need for disciplinary action on exceptional occasions as part of the authority given by Christ to his ministers, however difficult it may be in practice to take such action. This is what we meant by saying that the bishop 'can require the compliance necessary to maintain faith and charity in its daily life' (para. 5). At the same time the authority of the ordained minister is not held in isolation, but is shared with other ministers and the rest of the community. All the ministers, whatever their role in the body of Christ, are involved in responsibility for preserving the integrity of the community.

Jurisdiction

6   Critics have asked for clarification on two matters.

First, what do we mean by jurisdiction? We understand jurisdiction as the authority or power (*potestas*) necessary for the effective fulfilment of an office. Its exercise and limits are determined by what that office involves (cf. Authority II, paras. 16—22).

In both our communions we find dioceses comprising a number of parishes, and groups of dioceses at the provincial, national or international level. All of these are under the oversight of a special *episcope* exercised by ministers with a shared responsibility for the overall care of the Church. Every form of jurisdiction given to those exercising such an *episcope* is to serve and strengthen both the *koinonia* in the community and that between different Christian communities.

Secondly, it has been questioned whether we imply that jurisdiction attached to different levels of *episcope*—even within the same order of ministry—is always to be exercised in an identical way. Critics give the example of the relation and possible conflict between metropolitans and local bishops. We believe that the problem is not basically that of jurisdiction but of the complementarity and harmonious working of these differing forms of *episcope* in the one body of Christ. Jurisdiction, being the power necessary for the fulfilment of an office, varies according to the specific functions of each form of *episcope*. That is why the use of this juridical vocabulary does not mean that we attribute to all those exercising *episcope* at different levels exactly the same canonical power (cf. Authority II, para. 16).

Regional Primacy

7   Concern has been voiced that the Commission's treatment of regional primacy is inadequate. In particular, reference has been made to the ancient tradition of patriarchates.

The Commission did not ignore this tradition in its treatment of the origins of primacy (cf. para. 10). It avoided specific terms such as 'metropolitan' and 'patriarch', but in speaking of bishops with a special responsibility of oversight in their regions, the Commission intended to point to the reality behind the historical terms used for this form of episcopal co-responsibility in both east and west. It also pointed to the contemporary development and importance of new forms of regional primacy in both our traditions, e.g. the elective presidencies of Roman Catholic episcopal conferences and certain elective primacies in the Anglican Communion.

Primacy and History

8   It has been alleged that the Commission commends the primacy of the Roman see solely on the basis of history. But the Commission's argument is more than historical (cf. para. 23).

According to Christian doctrine the unity in truth of the Christian community demands visible expression. We agree that such visible expression is the will of God and that the maintenance of visible unity at the universal level includes the *episcope* of a universal primate. This is a doctrinal statement. But the way *episcope* is realized concretely in ecclesial life (the balance fluctuating between conciliarity and primacy) will depend upon contingent historical factors and upon development under the guidance of the Holy Spirit.

Though it is possible to conceive a universal primacy located elsewhere than in the city of Rome, the original witness of Peter and Paul and the continuing exercise of a universal *episcope* by the see of Rome present a unique presumption in its favour (cf. Authority II, paras. 6–9). Therefore, while to locate a universal primacy in the see of Rome is an affirmation at a different level from the assertion of the necessity for a universal primacy, it cannot be dissociated from the providential action of the Holy Spirit.

The design of God through the Holy Spirit has, we believe, been to preserve at once the fruitful diversity within the *koinonia* of local churches and the unity in essentials which must mark the universal *koinonia*. The history of our separation has underlined and continues to underline the necessity for this proper theological balance, which has often been distorted or destroyed by human failings or other historical factors (cf. para. 22).

The Commission does not therefore say that what has evolved historically or what is currently practised by the Roman see is necessarily normative: it maintains only that visible unity requires the realization of a 'general pattern of the complementary primatial and conciliar aspects of *episcope*' in the service of the universal '*koinonia* of the churches' (para. 23). Indeed much Anglican objection has been directed against the manner of the exercise and particular claims of the Roman primacy rather than against universal primacy as such.

Anglicanism has never rejected the principle and practice of primacy. New reflection upon it has been stimulated by the evolving role of the archbishop of Canterbury within the Anglican Communion. The development of this form of primacy arose precisely from the need for a service of unity in the faith in an expanding communion of Churches. It finds expression in the Lambeth Conferences convoked by successive archbishops of Canterbury which originated with requests from overseas provinces for guidance in matters of faith. This illustrates a particular relationship between conciliarity and primacy in the Anglican Communion.

The Commission has already pointed to the possibilities of mutual benefit and reform which should arise from a shared recognition of one universal primacy which does not inhibit conciliarity—a 'prospect (which) should be met with faith, not fear' (Co-Chairmen's Preface).

Anglicans sometimes fear the prospect of over-centralization, Roman Catholics the prospect of doctrinal incoherence. Faith, banishing fear, might see simply the prospect of the right balance between a primacy serving the unity and a conciliarity maintaining the just diversity of the *koinonia* of all the churches.

Authority in the Church   II

The Statement (1981)

Introduction

1   In our conclusion to our first Statement on Authority in the Church we affirmed that we had reached 'a consensus on authority in the Church and, in particular, on the basic principles of primacy', which we asserted to be of 'fundamental importance' (para. 24). Nevertheless we showed that four outstanding problems related to this subject required further study since, if they remained unresolved, they would appear to constitute serious obstacles to our growing together towards full communion. The four difficulties were the interpretation of the Petrine texts, the meaning of the language of 'divine right', the affirmation of papal infallibility, and the nature of the jurisdiction ascribed to the bishop of Rome as universal primate. After five years of further study we are able to present a fresh appraisal of their weight and implications.

Petrine Texts

2   The position of Peter among the apostles has often been discussed in relation to the importance of the bishop of Rome among the bishops. This requires that we look at the data of the New Testament and what are commonly called the Petrine texts.

3   While explicitly stressing Christ's will to root the Church in the apostolic witness and mandate, the New Testament attributes to Peter a special position among the Twelve. Whether the Petrine texts contain the authentic words of Jesus or not, they witness to an early tradition that Peter already held this place during Jesus' ministry. Individually the indications may seem to be inconclusive,

but taken together they provide a general picture of his prominence. The most important are: the bestowal on Simon of the name Cephas, his being mentioned first among the Twelve and in the smaller circle of the three (Peter, James and John), the faith which enabled him to confess Jesus' Messiahship (Matt. 16.16; Mark 8.29; Luke 9.20; and John 6.69), and the answer of Jesus (Matt. 16.18) in which he is called rock, the charge to strengthen his brethren (Luke 22.31−32) and to feed the sheep (John 21. 16−17) and the special appearance to him of the risen Lord (e.g. Luke 24.34; 1 Cor. 15.5). Although the author of Acts underlined the apostolic authority of Paul in the latter part of his book, he focused in the first part on Peter's leadership. For instance, it is Peter who frequently speaks in the name of the apostolic community (Acts 3.15, 10.41), he is the first to proclaim the Gospel to the Jews and the first to open the Christian community to the Gentiles. Paul seems to have recognized this prominence of Peter among the apostles as well as the importance of James (Gal. 1.18−19). He appears also to have accepted the lead given by Peter at the Council of Jerusalem (Acts 15), even though he was prepared to oppose Peter when he held Peter to be at fault (Gal. 2.11).

4   Responsibility for pastoral leadership was not restricted to Peter. The expression 'binding and loosing', which is used for the explicit commission to Peter in Matt. 16.19, appears again in Matt. 18.18 in the promise made by Christ directly to all the disciples. Similarly the foundation upon which the Church is built is related to Peter in Matt. 16.18 and to the whole apostolic body elsewhere in the New Testament (e.g. Eph. 2.20). Even though Peter was the spokesman at Pentecost, the charge to proclaim the Gospel to all the world had previously been given by the risen Christ to the Eleven (Acts 1.2−8).

Although Paul was not among the Twelve, he too was conspicuous for the leadership which he exercised with an authority received from the Lord himself, claiming to share with Peter and others parallel responsibility and apostolic authority (Gal. 2.7—8; 1 Cor. 9.1).

5   In spite of being strongly rebuked by Christ and his dramatic failure in denying him, in the eyes of the New Testament writers Peter holds a position of special importance. This was not due to his own gifts and character although he had been the first to confess Christ's Messiahship. It was because of his particular calling by Christ (Luke 6.14; John 21.15—17). Yet while the distinctive features of Peter's ministry are stressed, this ministry is that of an apostle and does not isolate him from the ministry of the other apostles. In accordance with the teaching of Jesus that truly to lead is to serve and not to dominate others (Luke 22.24ff), Peter's role in strengthening the brethren (Luke 22.32) is a leadership of service. Peter, then, serves the Church by helping it to overcome threats to its unity (e.g. Acts 11.1—18), even if his weakness may require help or correction, as is clear from his rebuke by Paul (Gal. 2.11—14). These considerations help clarify the analogy that has been drawn between the role of Peter among the apostles and that of the bishop of Rome among his fellow bishops.

6   The New Testament contains no explicit record of a transmission of Peter's leadership; nor is the transmission of apostolic authority in general very clear. Furthermore, the Petrine texts were subjected to differing interpretations as early as the time of the Church Fathers. Yet the church at Rome, the city in which Peter and Paul taught and were martyred, came to be recognized as possessing a unique responsibility among the churches: its bishop was seen to perform a special service in relation to the unity of the

churches, and in relation to fidelity to the apostolic inheritance, thus exercising among his fellow bishops functions analogous to those ascribed to Peter, whose successor the bishop of Rome was claimed to be (cf. para. 12).

7   Fathers and doctors of the Church gradually came to interpret the New Testament data as pointing in the same direction. This interpretation has been questioned, and it has been argued that it arose from an attempt to legitimize a development which had already occurred. Yet it is possible to think that a primacy of the bishop of Rome is not contrary to the New Testament and is part of God's purpose regarding the Church's unity and catholicity, while admitting that the New Testament texts offer no sufficient basis for this.

8   Our two traditions agree that not everything said of the apostles as the witnesses to the resurrection and saving work of Christ (Acts 1.21–22) is transmitted to those chosen to continue their mission. The apostles are the foundations precisely because they are the unique, commissioned witnesses to the once-for-all saving work of Christ. Peter's role is never isolated from that of the apostolic group; what is true of the transmissibility of the mission of the apostolic group is true of Peter as a member of it. Consequently though the sentence, 'On this rock I will build my church', is spoken to Peter, this does not imply that the same words can be applied to the bishop of Rome with an identical meaning. Even if Peter's role cannot be transmitted in its totality, however, this does not exclude the continuation of a ministry of unity guided by the Spirit among those who continue the apostolic mission.

9   If the leadership of the bishop of Rome has been rejected by those who thought it was not faithful to the

truth of the Gospel and hence not a true focus of unity, we nevertheless agree that a universal primacy will be needed in a reunited Church and should appropriately be the primacy of the bishop of Rome, as we have specified it (Authority I, para. 23). While the New Testament taken as a whole shows Peter playing a clear role of leadership it does not portray the Church's unity and universality exclusively in terms of Peter. The universal communion of the churches is a company of believers, united by faith in Christ, by the preaching of the word, and by participation in the sacraments assured to them by a pastoral ministry of apostolic order. In a reunited Church a ministry modelled on the role of Peter will be a sign and safeguard of such unity.

Jus Divinum

10   The first Statement on Authority poses two questions with respect to the language of 'divine right' applied by the First Vatican Council to the Roman primacy: What does the language actually mean? What implications does it have for the ecclesial status of non-Roman Catholic communions (Authority I, para. 24*b*)? Our purpose is to clarify the Roman Catholic position on these questions; to suggest a possible Anglican reaction to the Roman Catholic position; and to attempt a statement of consensus.

11   The Roman Catholic conviction concerning the place of the Roman primacy in God's plan for his Church has traditionally been expressed in the language of *jus divinum* (divine law or divine right). This term was used by the First Vatican Council to describe the primacy of the 'successor in the chair of Peter' whom the Council recognized in the bishop of Rome. The First Vatican Council used the term *jure divino* to say that this primacy

derives from Christ.[1] While there is no universally accepted interpretation of this language, all affirm that it means at least that this primacy expresses God's purpose for his Church. *Jus divinum* in this context need not be taken to imply that the universal primacy as a permanent institution was directly founded by Jesus during his life on earth. Neither does the term mean that the universal primate is a 'source of the Church' as if Christ's salvation had to be channelled through him. Rather, he is to be the sign of the visible *koinonia* God wills for the Church and an instrument through which unity in diversity is realized. It is to a universal primate thus envisaged within the collegiality of the bishops and the *koinonia* of the whole Church that the qualification *jure divino* can be applied.

12   The doctrine that a universal primacy expresses the will of God does not entail the consequence that a Christian community out of communion with the see of Rome does not belong to the Church of God. Being in canonical communion with the bishop of Rome is not among the necessary elements by which a Christian community is recognized as a church. For example, the Roman Catholic Church has continued to recognize the Orthodox churches as churches in spite of division concerning the primacy (Vatican II, *Unitatis Redintegratio*, para. 14). The Second Vatican Council, while teaching that the Church of God subsists in the Roman Catholic Church, rejected the position that the Church of God is co-extensive with the Roman Catholic Church and is exclusively embodied in that Church. The Second Vatican Council allows it to be said that a church out of communion with the Roman see may lack nothing from the viewpoint of the Roman Catholic Church except that it does not belong to the visible manifestation of full

[1] 'ex ipsius Christi Domini institutione seu iure divino' (*Pastor Aeternus*, ch. 2).

Christian communion which is maintained in the Roman Catholic Church (*Lumen Gentium*, para. 8; *Unitatis Redintegratio*, para. 13).

13 Relations between our two communions in the past have not encouraged reflection by Anglicans on the positive significance of the Roman primacy in the life of the universal Church. Nonetheless, from time to time Anglican theologians have affirmed that, in changed circumstances, it might be possible for the churches of the Anglican Communion to recognize the development of the Roman primacy as a gift of divine providence—in other words, as an effect of the guidance of the Holy Spirit in the Church. Given the above interpretation of the language of divine right in the First Vatican Council, it is reasonable to ask whether a gap really exists between the assertion of a primacy by divine right (*jure divino*) and the acknowledgement of its emergence by divine providence (*divina providentia*).

14 Anglicans have commonly supposed that the claim to divine right for the Roman primacy implied a denial that the churches of the Anglican Communion are churches. Consequently, they have concluded that any reconciliation with Rome would require a repudiation of their past history, life and experience—which in effect would be a betrayal of their own integrity. However, given recent developments in the Roman Catholic understanding of the status of other Christian churches, this particular difficulty may no longer be an obstacle to Anglican acceptance, as God's will for his Church, of a universal primacy of the bishop of Rome such as has been described in the first Statement on Authority (para. 23).

15 In the past, Roman Catholic teaching that the bishop of Rome is universal primate by divine right or law has

been regarded by Anglicans as unacceptable. However, we believe that the primacy of the bishop of Rome can be affirmed as part of God's design for the universal *koinonia* in terms which are compatible with both our traditions. Given such a consensus, the language of divine right used by the First Vatican Council need no longer be seen as a matter of disagreement between us.

Jurisdiction

16 Jurisdiction in the Church may be defined as the authority or power (*potestas*) necessary for the exercise of an office. In both our communions it is given for the effective fulfilment of office and this fact determines its exercise and limits. It varies according to the specific functions of the *episcope* concerned. The jurisdictions associated with different levels of *episcope* (e.g. of primates, metropolitans and diocesan bishops) are not in all respects identical.

The use of the same juridical terms does not mean that exactly the same authority is attributed to all those exercising *episcope* at different levels. Where a metropolitan has jurisdiction in his province this jurisdiction is not merely the exercise in a broader context of that exercised by a bishop in his diocese: it is determined by the specific functions which he is required to discharge in relation to his fellow bishops.

17 Each bishop is entrusted with the pastoral authority needed for the exercise of his *episcope*. This authority is both required and limited by the bishop's task of teaching the faith through the proclamation and explanation of the word of God, of providing for the administration of the sacraments in his diocese and of maintaining his church in holiness and truth (cf. Authority I, para. 5). Hence decisions taken by the bishop in performing his task have

an authority which the faithful in his diocese have a duty to accept. This authority of the bishop, usually called jurisdiction, involves the responsibility for making and implementing the decisions that are required by his office for the sake of the *koinonia*. It is not the arbitrary power of one man over the freedom of others, but a necessity if the bishop is to serve his flock as its shepherd (cf. Authority Elucidation, para. 5). So too, within the universal *koinonia* and the collegiality of the bishops, the universal primate exercises the jurisdiction necessary for the fulfilment of his functions, the chief of which is to serve the faith and unity of the whole Church.

18 Difficulties have arisen from the attribution of universal, ordinary and immediate jurisdiction to the bishop of Rome by the First Vatican Council. Misunderstanding of these technical terms has aggravated the difficulties. The jurisdiction of the bishop of Rome as universal primate is called ordinary and immediate (i.e. not mediated) because it is inherent in his office; it is called universal simply because it must enable him to serve the unity and harmony of the *koinonia* as a whole and in each of its parts.

The attribution of such jurisdiction to the bishop of Rome is a source of anxiety to Anglicans (Authority I, para. 24d) who fear, for example, that he could usurp the rights of a metropolitan in his province or of a bishop in his diocese; that a centralized authority might not always understand local conditions or respect legitimate cultural diversity; that rightful freedom of conscience, thought and action could be imperilled.

19 The universal primate should exercise, and be seen to exercise, his ministry not in isolation but in collegial association with his brother bishops (Authority I, paras. 21 and 23). This in no way reduces his own responsibility

on occasion to speak and act for the whole Church. Concern for the universal Church is intrinsic to all episcopal office; a diocesan bishop is helped to make this concern a reality by the universal jurisdiction of the universal primate. But the universal primate is not the source from which diocesan bishops derive their authority, nor does his authority undermine that of the metropolitan or diocesan bishop. Primacy is not an autocratic power over the Church but a service in and to the Church which is a communion in faith and charity of local churches.

20 Although the scope of universal jurisdiction cannot be precisely defined canonically, there are moral limits to its exercise: they derive from the nature of the Church and of the universal primate's pastoral office. By virtue of his jurisdiction, given for the building up of the Church, the universal primate has the right in special cases to intervene in the affairs of a diocese and to receive appeals from the decision of a diocesan bishop. It is because the universal primate, in collegial association with his fellow bishops, has the task of safeguarding the faith and unity of the universal Church that the diocesan bishop is subject to his authority.

21 The purpose of the universal primate's jurisdiction is to enable him to further catholicity as well as unity and to foster and draw together the riches of the diverse traditions of the churches. Collegial and primatial responsibility for preserving the distinctive life of the local churches involves a proper respect for their customs and traditions, provided these do not contradict the faith or disrupt communion. The search for unity and concern for catholicity must not be divorced.

22 Even though these principles concerning the nature

of jurisdiction be accepted as in line with the understanding which Anglicans and Roman Catholics share
with regard to the Church's structure, there remain
specific questions about their practical application in a
united Church. Anglicans are entitled to assurance that
acknowledgement of the universal primacy of the bishop
of Rome would not involve the suppression of theological,
liturgical and other traditions which they value or the
imposition of wholly alien traditions. We believe that what
has been said above provides grounds for such assurance.
In this connection we recall the words of Paul VI in 1970:
'There will be no seeking to lessen the legitimate prestige
and the worthy patrimony of piety and usage proper to the
Anglican Church. . .'[2]

Infallibility

23   It is Christ himself, the Way, the Truth and the Life,
who entrusts the Gospel to us and gives to his Church
teaching authority which claims our obedience. The
Church as a whole, indwelt by the Spirit according to
Christ's promise and looking to the testimony of the
prophets, saints and martyrs of every generation, is
witness, teacher and guardian of the truth (cf. Authority I,
para. 18). The Church is confident that the Holy Spirit
will effectually enable it to fulfil its mission so that it will
neither lose its essential character nor fail to reach its
goal.[3] We are agreed that doctrinal decisions made

[2] There will be no seeking to lessen the legitimate prestige and the worthy
patrimony of piety and usage proper to the Anglican Church when the Roman
Catholic Church—this humble "Servant of the servants of God"—is able to
embrace her ever beloved Sister in the one authentic communion of the family
of Christ. . .' (AAS 62 (1970), p. 753).

[3] This is the meaning of *indefectibility*, a term which does not speak of the
Church's lack of defects but confesses that, despite all its many weaknesses
and failures, Christ is faithful to his promise that the gates of hell shall not
prevail against it.

by legitimate authority must be consonant with the community's faith as grounded in Scripture and interpreted by the mind of the Church, and that no teaching authority can add new revelation to the original apostolic faith (cf. Authority I, paras. 2 and 18). We must then ask whether there is a special ministerial gift of discerning the truth and of teaching bestowed at crucial times on one person to enable him to speak authoritatively in the name of the Church in order to preserve the people of God in the truth.

24 Maintenance in the truth requires that at certain moments the Church can in a matter of essential doctrine make a decisive judgement which becomes part of its permanent witness.[4] Such a judgement makes it clear what the truth is, and strengthens the Church's confidence in proclaiming the Gospel. Obvious examples of such judgements are occasions when general councils define the faith. These judgements, by virtue of their foundation in revelation and their appropriateness to the need of the time, express a renewed unity in the truth to which they summon the whole Church.

25 The Church in all its members is involved in such a definition which clarifies and enriches their grasp of the truth. Their active reflection upon the definition in its turn clarifies its significance. Moreover, although it is not through reception by the people of God that a definition first acquires authority, the assent of the faithful is the ultimate indication that the Church's authoritative decision in a matter of faith has been truly preserved from error by the Holy Spirit. The Holy Spirit who maintains the Church in the truth will bring its members to receive the definition as true and to assimilate it if what has been declared genuinely expounds the revelation.

[4] That this is in line with Anglican belief is clear from the Thirty-nine Articles (Article 20): 'The Church hath . . . authority in Controversies of Faith'.

26   The Church exercises teaching authority through various instruments and agencies at various levels (cf. Authority I, paras. 9 and 18—22). When matters of faith are at stake decisions may be made by the Church in universal councils; we are agreed that these are authoritative (cf. Authority I, para. 19). We have also recognized the need in a united Church for a universal primate who, presiding over the *koinonia*, can speak with authority in the name of the Church (cf. Authority I, para. 23). Through both these agencies the Church can make a decisive judgement in matters of faith, and so exclude error.

27   The purpose of this service cannot be to add to the content of revelation, but is to recall and emphasize some important truth; to expound the faith more lucidly; to expose error; to draw out implications not sufficiently recognized; and to show how Christian truth applies to contemporary issues. These statements would be intended to articulate, elucidate or define matters of faith which the community believes at least implicitly. The welfare of the *koinonia* does not require that all the statements of those who speak authoritatively on behalf of the Church should be considered permanent expressions of the truth. But situations may occur where serious divisions of opinion on crucial issues of pastoral urgency call for a more definitive judgement. Any such statement would be intended as an expression of the mind of the Church, understood not only in the context of its time and place but also in the light of the Church's whole experience and tradition. All such definitions are provoked by specific historical situations and are always made in terms of the understanding and framework of their age (cf. Authority I, para. 15). But in the continuing life of the Church they retain a lasting significance if they are safeguarding the substance of the faith.

G

The Church's teaching authority is a service to which the faithful look for guidance especially in times of uncertainty; but the assurance of the truthfulness of its teaching rests ultimately rather upon its fidelity to the Gospel than upon the character or office of the person by whom it is expressed. The Church's teaching is proclaimed because it is true; it is not true simply because it has been proclaimed. The value of such authoritative proclamation lies in the guidance that it gives to the faithful. However, neither general councils nor universal primates are invariably preserved from error even in official declarations (cf. Authority Elucidation, para. 3).

28   The Church's judgement is normally given through synodal decision, but at times a primate acting in communion with his fellow bishops may articulate the decision even apart from a synod. Although responsibility for preserving the Church from fundamental error belongs to the whole Church, it may be exercised on its behalf by a universal primate. The exercise of authority in the Church need not have the effect of stifling the freedom of the Spirit to inspire other agencies and individuals. In fact, there have been times in the history of the Church when both councils and universal primates have protected legitimate positions which have been under attack.

29   A service of preserving the Church from error has been performed by the bishop of Rome as universal primate both within and outside the synodal process. The judgement of Leo I, for example, in his letter received by the Council of Chalcedon, helped to maintain a balanced view of the two natures in Christ. This does not mean that other bishops are restricted to a merely consultative role, nor that every statement of the bishop of Rome instantly solves the immediate problem or decides the matter at issue for ever. To be a decisive discernment of the truth,

the judgement of the bishop of Rome must satisfy rigorous conditions. He must speak explicitly as the focus within the *koinonia*; without being under duress from external pressures; having sought to discover the mind of his fellow bishops and of the Church as a whole; and with a clear intention to issue a binding decision upon a matter of faith or morals. Some of these conditions were laid down by the First Vatican Council.[5] When it is plain that all these conditions have been fulfilled, Roman Catholics conclude that the judgement is preserved from error and the proposition true. If the definition proposed for assent were not manifestly a legitimate interpretation of biblical faith and in line with orthodox tradition, Anglicans would think it a duty to reserve the reception of the definition for study and discussion.

30   This approach is illustrated by the reaction of many Anglicans to the Marian definitions, which are the only examples of such dogmas promulgated by the bishop of Rome apart from a synod since the separation of our two communions. Anglicans and Roman Catholics can agree in much of the truth that these two dogmas are designed to affirm. We agree that there can be but one mediator between God and man, Jesus Christ, and reject any interpretation of the role of Mary which obscures this affirmation. We agree in recognizing that Christian understanding of Mary is inseparably linked with the doctrines of Christ and of the Church. We agree in recognizing the

---

[5] The phrase 'eiusmodi ... definitiones ex sese, non autem ex consensu ecclesiae irreformabiles esse': 'such definitions are irreformable by themselves and not by reason of the agreement of the Church' (*Pastor Aeternus*, ch. 4) does not deny the importance of reception of doctrinal statements in the Roman Catholic Church. The phrase was used by the Council to rule out the opinion of those who maintained that such a statement becomes 'irreformable' only subsequently when it is approved by the bishops. The term 'irreformable' means that the truth expressed in the definition can no longer be questioned. 'Irreformable' does not mean that the definition is the Church's last word on the matter and that the definition cannot be restated in other terms.

grace and unique vocation of Mary, Mother of God Incarnate (*Theotokos*), in observing her festivals, and in according her honour in the communion of saints. We agree that she was prepared by divine grace to be the mother of our Redeemer, by whom she herself was redeemed and received into glory. We further agree in recognizing in Mary a model of holiness, obedience and faith for all Christians. We accept that it is possible to regard her as a prophetic figure of the Church of God before as well as after the Incarnation.[6] Nevertheless the dogmas of the Immaculate Conception and the Assumption raise a special problem for those Anglicans who do not consider that the precise definitions given by these dogmas are sufficiently supported by Scripture. For many Anglicans the teaching authority of the bishop of Rome, independent of a council, is not recommended by the fact that through it these Marian doctrines were proclaimed as dogmas binding on all the faithful. Anglicans would also ask whether, in any future union between our two Churches, they would be required to subscribe to such dogmatic statements. One consequence of our separation has been a tendency for Anglicans and Roman Catholics alike to exaggerate the importance of the Marian dogmas in themselves at the expense of other truths more closely related to the foundation of the Christian faith.

31   In spite of our agreement over the need of a universal primacy in a united Church, Anglicans do not accept the guaranteed possession of such a gift of divine assistance in

---

[6] The affirmation of the Roman Catholic Church that Mary was conceived without original sin is based on recognition of her unique role within the mystery of the Incarnation. By being thus prepared to be the mother of our Redeemer, she also becomes a sign that the salvation won by Christ was operative among all mankind before his birth. The affirmation that her glory in heaven involves full participation in the fruits of salvation expresses and reinforces our faith that the life of the world to come has already broken into the life of our world. It is the conviction of Roman Catholics that the Marian dogmas formulate a faith consonant with Scripture.

judgement necessarily attached to the office of the bishop of Rome by virtue of which his formal decisions can be known to be wholly assured before their reception by the faithful. Nevertheless the problem about reception is inherently difficult. It would be incorrect to suggest that in controversies of faith no conciliar or papal definition possesses a right to attentive sympathy and acceptance until it has been examined by every individual Christian and subjected to the scrutiny of his private judgement. We agree that, without a special charism guarding the judgement of the universal primate, the Church would still possess means of receiving and ascertaining the truth of revelation. This is evident in the acknowledged gifts of grace and truth in churches not in full communion with the Roman see.

32   Roman Catholic tradition has used the term infallibility to describe guaranteed freedom from fundamental error in judgement.[7] We agree that this is a term applicable unconditionally only to God, and that to use it of a human being, even in highly restricted circumstances, can produce many misunderstandings. That is why in stating our belief in the preservation of the Church from error we have avoided using the term. We also recognize that the ascription to the bishop of Rome of infallibility under certain conditions has tended to lend exaggerated importance to all his statements.

33   We have already been able to agree that conciliarity and primacy are complementary (Authority I, paras. 22—23). We can now together affirm that the Church needs both a multiple, dispersed authority, with which all God's

---

[7] In Roman Catholic doctrine, *infallibility* means only the preservation of the judgement from error for the maintenance of the Church in the truth, not positive inspiration or revelation. Moreover the infallibility ascribed to the bishop of Rome is a gift to be, in certain circumstances and under precise conditions, an organ of the infallibility of the Church.

people are actively involved, and also a universal primate as servant and focus of visible unity in truth and love. This does not mean that all differences have been eliminated; but if any Petrine function and office are exercised in the living Church of which a universal primate is called to serve as a visible focus, then it inheres in his office that he should have both a defined teaching responsibility and appropriate gifts of the Spirit to enable him to discharge it.

Contemporary discussions of conciliarity and primacy in both communions indicate that we are not dealing with positions destined to remain static. We suggest that some difficulties will not be wholly resolved until a practical initiative has been taken and our two Churches have lived together more visibly in the one *koinonia*.

Conclusion

This Final Report of the Anglican—Roman Catholic International Commission represents a significant stage in relations between the Anglican Communion and the Roman Catholic Church. The decision by our respective authorities, made as long ago as 1966, to enter into serious dialogue in order to resolve long-standing issues which have been at the origin of our separation, resulted in our concentration on three main areas of controversy: the doctrine of the eucharist, ministry and ordination, and the nature and exercise of authority in the Church.

This dialogue, however, has been directed not merely to the achievement of doctrinal agreement, which is central to our reconciliation, but to the far greater goal of organic unity. The convergence reflected in our Final Report would appear to call for the establishing of a new relationship between our Churches as a next stage in the journey towards Christian unity.

We understand but do not share the fears of those who think that such Statements constitute a threat to all that is distinctive and true in their own traditions. It is our hope to carry with us in the substance of our agreement not only Roman Catholics and Anglicans but all Christians, and that what we have done may contribute to the visible unity of all the people of God as well as to the reconciliation of our two Churches.

We are well aware of how much we owe to others and of how much we have left others still to do. Our agreement still needs to be tested, but in 1981 it has become abundantly clear that, under the Holy Spirit, our Churches have grown closer together in faith and charity. There are high expectations that significant initiatives will be boldly undertaken to deepen our reconciliation and lead us forward in the quest for the full communion to which we have been committed, in obedience to God, from the beginning of our dialogue.

Appendices

Meetings of the Commission

1 *The first meeting of the Anglican—Roman Catholic International Commission took place at St George's House, Windsor Castle, 9—15 January 1970.* The Commission, following the Malta Report, examined eucharist, ministry and authority in relation to the overall concept of *koinonia*. Anglican and Roman Catholic position papers had been prepared in advance on all three subjects.

2 *The second meeting took place in Venice, 21—28 September 1970 at the Fondazione Cini on the Isola San Giorgio.* Preparatory papers on authority had been prepared by members in Oxford, a Roman Catholic position paper on ministry was presented from the USA and a working paper on the eucharist from the South African Anglican—Roman Catholic Commission. Working papers on Eucharist, Ministry and Authority were published from this meeting in *Theology* (February 1971), *Clergy Review* (February 1971), and *One in Christ* (2—3 1971) but only carried the authority of the respective sub-commissions which were responsible for them. Consideration was also given to questions of moral theology, and three consultants presented papers to the Commission. However, pressure of the main work of the Commission prevented them being pursued, and it was decided that from then on the Commission should concentrate on one subject at a time.

3 *The Commission returned to St George's House, Windsor Castle, for its third meeting, 1—8 September 1971.* A collection of short papers on eucharistic sacrifice had been prepared for this meeting in Oxford. Anglican and Roman Catholic position papers on the real presence were offered from Canada and a sub-commission met at Poringland, Norwich, 12—16 April 1971, which prepared a draft statement on the eucharist. At Windsor the Commission worked in three sub-commissions on the Poringland draft, concentrating on the problems of presence and sacrifice. After redrafting, the Commission completed its *Agreed Statement on Eucharistic Doctrine* and it was published on 31 December 1971, with the permission of the authorities of the two Churches. Social and cultural factors were also considered at this meeting, and the Commission received a paper presented by a sociological consultant.

4 *The next meeting took place at the Villa Cagnola, Gazzada, Italy, 30 August—7 September 1972.* Short preparatory papers on ministry in the New Testament had been prepared in Oxford, and a Roman Catholic paper on *Sacerdotium* was offered from Canada. A number of papers, both Anglican and Roman Catholic, were written in the USA on bishops and priests, and a paper on the problem of orders was prepared in South Africa. A sub-commission met in Woodstock College, New York, 22—26 May 1972 to consider all this preparatory material. At Gazzada the Commission produced two draft texts on ministry in the New Testament and on apostolicity.

5 *The fifth meeting took place in Canterbury, 28 August—6 September 1973 at St Augustine's College.* In preparation for this meeting there had been joint work on apostolic succession in Oxford, on priesthood in Montreal and on ordination in

South Africa. A sub-commission met at Poringland, Norwich, 11–15 June 1973 at which all the preparatory material was reviewed, including that from the previous full meeting, and a draft statement on ministry and ordination was offered to the full Commission. At Canterbury the Poringland draft was revised and elaborated and its major themes were accepted: ministries in the life of the Church (including ministry in the New Testament and early Church), the ordained ministry (including the use of priestly language) and ordination (including apostolic succession). The Statement *Ministry and Ordination* was then accepted. It was published on 13 December 1973, with the permission of the respective authorities, and included a historical appendix by the then Anglican Co-Secretary, the Revd Colin Davey.

6 *At the Centro Mariapoli, Grottaferrata, Italy, 27 August–5 September 1974, the Commission reverted to the issue of authority.* Material on the authority of the Bible had been prepared in South Africa, on *koinonia* and ecclesiology in the USA and on the ecclesiology of Vatican II in Oxford. The English Anglican–Roman Catholic Commission also prepared material on indefectibility and infallibility. There were also important position papers by individual members of the Commission on schism, on magisterium in the early Church, on Vatican I, and on the *sensus fidelium*. The main work of the full Commission that year centred on the authority of Scripture and on the role of the *sensus fidelium*. On 3 September the Commission was received in audience by Pope Paul VI at Castelgandolfo.

7 *The next meeting of the Commission took place in Oxford at St Stephen's House, 29 August–5 September 1975.* To prepare for this meeting a small sub-commission met at Poringland, Norwich, 11–15 December 1974 which revised drafts from the previous meeting. A further sub-commission met at the Royal Foundation of St Katharine, Stepney, London, 22–26 June 1975 which continued the work of the Poringland meeting and offered the full Commission a draft text on the lordship of Christ, the authority of the Scriptures, the *sensus fidelium* and the authority conferred by holiness and by special gifts of the Spirit. The full Commission also had before it four important position papers: two Anglican papers on the exercise of authority in the Church and on the relation between truth and authority, and two Roman Catholic papers on the primacy of the bishop of Rome and on jurisdiction. The full Commission scrutinized the St Katharine's draft but refrained from amending it at that stage. Instead it continued the logic of the draft by dividing into two sub-commissions to deal with primacy in relation to unity, and infallibility and truth in relation to councils. On 3 September the Commission was joined by the Archbishop of Canterbury, Dr Donald Coggan.

8 *The Commission returned to Venice for its eighth meeting, staying at the Casa Cardinale Piazza, Madonna dell' Orto, 24 August–2 September 1976.* A small sub-commission had again met at Poringland, Norwich, 9–12 February 1976. It put together the draft material on unity and truth from the two sub-commissions at the Oxford meeting. A larger sub-commission met later at Hengrave Hall, Bury St Edmunds, 21–25 June 1976 and after revision of the Poringland material added new material on primacy, collegiality and conciliarity. The full Commission therefore had an extended draft statement on authority before it. Sub-commissions at Venice then revised the new material from Poringland and Hengrave, with separate attention to the question of the development of doctrine and decisions in matters of faith. The whole draft was revised, an important conclusion added, and the Commission finally accepted the *Agreed Statement on Authority in the Church*. It was published on 20 January 1977, with the permission of the two authorities.

9 *The next meeting was at Chichester Theological College, 30 August—8 September 1977.* It had been decided that this meeting should be devoted to responding to criticisms of the Agreed Statements and papers were prepared cataloguing both Anglican and Roman Catholic criticisms. At Chichester it was decided to elucidate the Statements rather than simply engage in debate and three sub-commissions began this task.

10 *Due to the death of Pope Paul VI the next meeting of the Commission did not take place till 12—20 January 1979 at Salisbury and Wells Theological College, Salisbury.* Meanwhile there had been a small sub-commission meeting at Damascus House, Mill Hill, London, 9—10 June 1978, which revised the Chichester material on the eucharist, and a large sub-commission met later in the year at All Saints' Pastoral Centre, London Colney, St Albans, 4—7 September (during part of the time when the full Commission would have been meeting) and completed a draft text on ministry and ordination. At Salisbury, therefore, the Commission revised the two texts and agreed to its response to criticisms of the first two Statements. *Elucidations* was published on 7 June 1979.

11 *The Commission resumed its discussion of authority at the Casa Cardinale Piazza, Madonna dell' Orto, Venice, 28 August—6 September 1979.* It had before it preliminary work on the four serious problems left unresolved at the conclusion of *Authority in the Church I* from a sub-commission which had met at Verulam House, St Albans a year earlier, 5—9 June 1978. It also had before it position papers by members which had been prepared in time for this sub-commission: a joint Anglican—Roman Catholic paper on the Petrine texts from the USA, an Anglican paper on the Spirit's abiding in the Church with a Roman Catholic response, joint notes on the problem of *jus divinum*, and a substantial Roman Catholic paper on the jurisdiction of the bishop of Rome. Two drafters had also prepared material to continue the earlier Statement. The Commission itself divided into four sub-commissions at Venice and four tentative drafts on the above subjects emerged.

12 *The twelfth meeting again took place in Venice at the Casa Cardinale Piazza, 26 August—4 September 1980.* The drafts from the previous meeting were criticized and refined. Material on the Petrine texts, *jus divinum* and jurisdiction was all but completed, but the draft on infallibility was unfinished. On 4 September the Commission was received in audience by Pope John Paul II at Castelgandolfo.

13 *The final meeting of the Commission took place at St George's House, Windsor Castle, 25 August—3 September 1981.* A draft introduction had been prepared over a year before by a sub-commission which had met at the Southwark Diocesan Training Centre, Wychcroft, Redhill, 7—11 January 1980. This draft expounded the

Commission's ecclesiology. Work had also begun in the same year on a response to criticisms of the first Statement on Authority by a sub-commission at the Cenacle Retreat and Conference Centre, Burnham, Slough, 22–26 June 1980. At a large sub-commission in Liverpool at St Katharine's College, 15–19 December 1980, the draft material on infallibility left unfinished at the previous full meeting in Venice was completed. The St Katharine's sub-commission also began revising the response to criticisms on Authority drafted at Burnham. A final sub-commission met at St Agnes' Retreat House, Bristol, 9–13 June 1981 and revised the introductory draft on the Church prepared at Wychcroft, stressing the Commission's use of *koinonia*, and completing the revision of the draft response to criticisms on authority. The final meeting at Windsor had therefore a full set of draft texts for scrutiny, criticism and revision. For the first part of the meeting the Commission worked in five sub-commissions on Petrine texts, *jus divinum*, jurisdiction, infallibility, and an authority elucidation. For the second part the Commission worked as a whole, except the infallibility sub-commission, putting together all the drafts, revising the Introduction, and accepting the Preface. Towards the close of the final meeting all the new texts were unanimously agreed. On 1 September the Commission was received at Lambeth Palace by the Archbishop of Canterbury, Dr Robert Runcie. The permission of both authorities was given for publication of the Final Report in January 1982.

Members of the Commission

ANGLICAN DELEGATES

The Most Revd Henry McAdoo, Archbishop of Dublin (Co-Chairman)

The Rt Revd Felix Arnott, formerly Archbishop of Brisbane, now Anglican Chaplain in Venice

The Rt Revd John Moorman, formerly Bishop of Ripon

The Rt Revd Edward Knapp-Fisher, Archdeacon of Westminster

The Rt Revd Arthur A. Vogel, Bishop of West Missouri

The Revd Professor Henry Chadwick, Regius Professor of Divinity, University of Cambridge

The Revd Julian Charley, Rector, St Peter's, Everton, and Warden of Shrewsbury House

The Revd Canon Eugene R. Fairweather, Keble Professor of Divinity, Trinity College, University of Toronto

The Revd Canon Howard Root, Director of the Anglican Centre in Rome

CONSULTANTS

The Revd Canon John Halliburton, Principal, Chichester Theological College

The Revd Dr Harry Smythe, formerly Director of the Anglican Centre, Rome

SECRETARIES

The Revd Colin Davey, Assistant Chaplain, Archbishop of Canterbury's Counsellors on Foreign Relations (*until July 1974*)

The Revd Christopher Hill, Assistant Chaplain, Archbishop of Canterbury's Counsellors on Foreign Relations (*from August 1974*)

ROMAN CATHOLIC DELEGATES

The Rt Revd Alan Clark, Bishop of East Anglia (Co-Chairman)

The Rt Revd Christopher Butler, OSB, Auxiliary Bishop of Westminster

The Revd Fr Barnabas Ahern, CP, Professor of Sacred Scripture, Rome

The Revd Fr Pierre Duprey, WF, Under Secretary, Vatican Secretariat for Promoting Christian Unity

The Revd Dr Herbert Ryan, SJ, Professor of Theology, Loyola Marymount University, Los Angeles

Professor John Scarisbrick, Professor of History, University of Warwick

The Revd Fr George H. Tavard, AA, Professor of Theology, Methodist Theological School, Delaware, Ohio

The Revd Fr Jean Tillard, OP, Professor of Dogmatic Theology, Dominican Faculty of Theology, Ottawa

The Revd Dr Edward Yarnold, SJ, Tutor in Theology, Campion Hall, Oxford

SECRETARY

The Rt Revd Mgr William Purdy, Staff Member, Vatican Secretariat for Promoting Christian Unity

WORLD COUNCIL OF CHURCHES OBSERVER

The Revd Dr Günther Gassmann, President, Lutherisches Kirchenamt, Hannover

The Malta Report

Report of the Anglican—Roman Catholic
Joint Preparatory Commission

I

1   The visit of the Archbishop of Canterbury to Pope
Paul VI in March 1966, and their decision to constitute an
Anglican—Roman Catholic Joint Preparatory Commission,
marked a new stage in relations between our two
Churches. The three meetings of the Commission, held
during 1967 at Gazzada, Huntercombe, and in Malta,
were characterized not only by a spirit of charity and
frankness, but also by a growing sense of urgency,
penitence, thankfulness, and purpose: of urgency, in
response to the pressure of God's will, apprehended as
well in the processes of history and the aspirations and
achievements of men in his world as in the life, worship,
witness, and service of his Church; of penitence, in the
conviction of our shared responsibility for cherishing
animosities and prejudices which for four hundred years
have kept us apart, and prevented our attempting to
understand or resolve our differences; of thankfulness for
the measure of unity which through baptism into Christ
we already share, and for our recent growth towards
greater unity and mutual understanding; of purpose, in
our determination that the work begun in us by God shall
be brought by his grace to fulfilment in the restoration of
his peace to his Church and his world.

2   The members of the Commission have completed the
preparatory work committed to them by compiling this
report which they submit for their consideration to His
Holiness the Pope and His Grace the Archbishop. The

Decree on Ecumenism recognizes that among the Western Communions separated from the Roman See the Churches of the Anglican Communion 'hold a special place'. We hope in humility that our work may so help to further reconciliation between Anglicans and Roman Catholics as also to promote the wider unity of all Christians in their common Lord. We share the hope and prayer expressed in the common declaration issued by the Pope and the Archbishop after their meeting that 'a serious dialogue founded on the Gospels and on the ancient common traditions may lead to that unity in truth for which Christ prayed'.

3   We record with great thankfulness our common faith in God our Father, in our Lord Jesus Christ, and in the Holy Spirit; our common baptism in the one Church of God; our sharing of the holy Scriptures, of the Apostles' and Nicene Creeds, the Chalcedonian definition, and the teaching of the Fathers; our common Christian inheritance for many centuries with its living traditions of liturgy, theology, spirituality, Church order, and mission.

4   Divergences since the sixteenth century have arisen not so much from the substance of this inheritance as from our separate ways of receiving it. They derive from our experience of its value and power, from our interpretation of its meaning and authority, from our formulation of its content, from our theological elaboration of what it implies, and from our understanding of the manner in which the Church should keep and teach the Faith. Further study is needed to distinguish between those differences which are merely apparent, and those which are real and require serious examination.

5   We agree that revealed Truth is given in holy Scripture and formulated in dogmatic definitions through thought-

forms and language which are historically conditioned. We are encouraged by the growing agreement of theologians in our two Communions on methods of interpreting this historical transmission of revelation. We should examine further and together both the way in which we assent to and apprehend dogmatic truths and the legitimate means of understanding and interpreting them theologically. Although we agree that doctrinal comprehensiveness must have its limits, we believe that diversity has an intrinsic value when used creatively rather than destructively.

6   In considering these questions within the context of the present situation of our two Communions, we propose particularly as matter for dialogue the following possible convergences of lines of thought: first, between the traditional Anglican distinction of internal and external communion and the distinction drawn by the Vatican Council between full and partial communion; secondly, between the Anglican distinction of fundamentals from non-fundamentals and the distinction implied by the Vatican Council's references to a 'hierarchy of truths' (Decree on Ecumenism, 11), to the difference between 'revealed truths' and 'the manner in which they are formulated' (Pastoral Constitution on the Church in the Modern World, 62), and to diversities in theological tradition being often 'complementary rather than conflicting' (Decree on Ecumenism, 17).

II

7   We recommend that the second stage in our growing together begin with an official and explicit affirmation of mutual recognition from the highest authorities of each Communion. It would acknowledge that both Com-

munions are at one in the faith that the Church is founded upon the revelation of God the Father, made known to us in the Person and work of Jesus Christ, who is present through the Holy Spirit in the Scriptures and his Church, and is the only Mediator between God and Man, the ultimate Authority for all our doctrine. Each accepts the basic truths set forth in the ecumenical Creeds and the common tradition of the ancient Church, although neither Communion is tied to a positive acceptance of all the beliefs and devotional practices of the other.

8   In every region where each Communion has a hierarchy, we propose an annual joint meeting of either the whole or some considerable representation of the two hierarchies.

9   In the same circumstances we further recommend:

(*a*) Constant consultation between committees concerned with pastoral and evangelistic problems including, where appropriate, the appointment of joint committees.

(*b*) Agreements for joint use of churches and other ecclesiastical buildings, both existing and to be built, wherever such use is helpful for one or other of the two Communions.

(*c*) Agreements to share facilities for theological education, with the hope that all future priests of each Communion should have attended some course taught by a professor of the other Communion. Arrangements should also be made where possible for temporary exchange of students.

(*d*)   Collaboration in projects and institutions of theological scholarship to be warmly encouraged.

10   Prayer in common has been recommended by the Decree on Ecumenism and provisions for this common

worship are to be found in the *Directory* (para. 56). We urge that they be implemented.

11   Our similar liturgical and spiritual traditions make extensive sharing possible and desirable; for example, in non-eucharistic services, the exploration of new forms of worship, and retreats in common. Religious orders of similar inspiration in the two Communions are urged to develop a special relationship.

12   Our closeness in the field of sacramental belief leads us further to recommend that on occasion the exchange of preachers for the homily during the celebration of the Eucharist be also permitted, without prejudice to the more general regulations contained in the *Directory*.

13   Since our liturgies are closely related by reason of their common source, the ferment of liturgical renewal and reform now engaging both our Communions provides an unprecedented opportunity for collaboration. We should co-operate, and not take unilateral action, in any significant changes in the seasons and major holy days of the Christian Year; and we should experiment together in the development of a common eucharistic lectionary. A matter of special urgency in view of the advanced stage of liturgical revision in both Communions is that we reach agreement on the vernacular forms of those prayers, hymns, and responses which our people share in common in their respective liturgies. We recommend that this be taken up without delay.

We are gratified that collaboration in this work has been initiated by the exchange of observers and consultants in many of our respective liturgical commissions. Especially in matters concerning the vernacular, we recommend that representatives of our two Communions (not excluding other Christian bodies with similar liturgical concerns) be associated on a basis of equality both in international and in national and regional committees assigned this responsibility.

14   We believe that joint or parallel statements from our Church leaders at international, national, and local level on urgent human issues can provide a valuable form of Christian witness.

15   In the field of missionary strategy and activity ecumenical understanding is both uniquely valuable and particularly difficult. Very little has hitherto been attempted in this field between our two Communions and, while our other recommendations of course apply to the young Churches and mission areas, we propose further the institution at international level of an official joint consultation to consider the difficulties involved and the co-operation which should be undertaken.

16   The increasing number of mixed marriages points to the need for a thorough investigation of the doctrine of marriage in its sacramental dimension, its ethical demands, its canonical status, and its pastoral implications. It is hoped that the work of the Joint Commission on Marriage will be promptly initiated and vigorously pursued, and that its recommendations will help to alleviate some of the difficulties caused by mixed marriages, to indicate acceptable changes in Church regulations, and to provide safeguards against the dangers which threaten to undermine family life in our time.

III

17   We cannot envisage in detail what may be the issues and demands of the final stage in our quest for the full, organic unity of our two Communions. We know only that we must be constant in prayer for the grace of the Holy

Spirit in order that we may be open to his guidance and judgement, and receptive to each other's faith and understanding. There remain fundamental theological and moral questions between us where we need immediately to seek together for reconciling answers. In this search we cannot escape the witness of our history; but we cannot resolve our differences by mere reconsideration of, and judgement upon, the past. We must press on in confident faith that new light will be given us to lead us to our goal.

18   The fulfilment of our aim is far from imminent. In these circumstances the question of accepting some measure of sacramental intercommunion apart from full visible unity is being raised on every side. In the minds of many Christians no issue is today more urgent. We cannot ignore this, but equally we cannot sanction changes touching the very heart of Church life, eucharistic communion, without being certain that such changes would be truly Christian. Such certainty cannot be reached without more and careful study of the theology implied.

19   We are agreed that among the conditions required for intercommunion are both a true sharing in faith and the mutual recognition of ministry. The latter presents a particular difficulty in regard to Anglican Orders according to the traditional judgement of the Roman Church. We believe that the present growing together of our two Communions and the needs of the future require of us a very serious consideration of this question in the light of modern theology. The theology of the ministry forms part of the theology of the Church and must be considered as such. It is only when sufficient agreement has been reached as to the nature of the priesthood and the meaning to be attached in this context to the word 'validity' that we could proceed, working always jointly, to

114

the application of this doctrine to the Anglican ministry of today. We would wish to re-examine historical events and past documents only to the extent that they can throw light upon the facts of the present situation.

20   In addition, a serious theological examination should be jointly undertaken on the nature of authority with particular reference to its bearing on the interpretation of the historic faith to which both our Communions are committed. Real or apparent differences between us come to the surface in such matters as the unity and indefectibility of the Church and its teaching authority, the Petrine primacy, infallibility, and Mariological definitions.

21   In continuation of the work done by our Commission, we recommend that it be replaced by a Permanent Joint Commission responsible (in co-operation with the Secretariat for Promoting Christian Unity and the Church of England Council on Foreign Relations in association with the Anglican Executive Officer) for the oversight of Roman Catholic—Anglican relations, and the co-ordination of future work undertaken together by our two Communions.

22   We also recommend the constitution of two joint sub-commissions, responsible to the Permanent Commission, to undertake two urgent and important tasks:

> ONE to examine the question of intercommunion, and the related matters of Church and Ministry;
> THE OTHER to examine the question of authority, its nature, exercise, and implications.

We consider it important that adequate money, secretarial assistance, and research facilities should be given to the Commission and its sub-commissions in order that their members may do their work with thoroughness and efficiency.

23   We also recommend joint study of moral theology to determine similarities and differences in our teaching and practice in this field.

24   In concluding our Report we cannot do better than quote the words of those by whom we were commissioned, and to whom, with respect, we now submit it:

In willing obedience to the command of Christ who bade His disciples love one another, they declare that, with His help, they wish to leave in the hands of the God of mercy all that in the past has been opposed to this precept of charity, and that they make their own the mind of the Apostle which he expressed in these words: 'Forgetting those things which are behind, and reaching forth unto those things which are before, I press towards the mark for the prize of the high calling of God in Christ Jesus' (Phil. 3.13—14).

> The Common Declaration by Pope Paul VI
> and the Archbishop of Canterbury
> 24 March 1966

Malta, 2 January 1968

The Common Declaration by Pope Paul VI and the Archbishop of Canterbury

ROME, SAINT PAUL WITHOUT-THE-WALLS, 24 MARCH 1966

In this city of Rome, from which Saint Augustine was sent by Saint Gregory to England and there founded the cathedral see of Canterbury, towards which the eyes of all Anglicans now turn as the centre of their Christian Communion, His Holiness Pope Paul VI and His Grace Michael Ramsey, Archbishop of Canterbury, representing the Anglican Communion, have met to exchange fraternal greetings.

At the conclusion of their meeting they give thanks to Almighty God Who by the action of the Holy Spirit has in these latter years created a new atmosphere of Christian fellowship between the Roman Catholic Church and the Churches of the Anglican Communion.

This encounter of the 23 March 1966 marks a new stage in the development of fraternal relations, based upon Christian charity, and of sincere efforts to remove the causes of conflict and to re-establish unity.

In willing obedience to the command of Christ who bade His disciples love one another, they declare that, with His help, they wish to leave in the hands of the God of mercy all that in the past has been opposed to this precept of charity, and that they make their own the mind of the Apostle which he expressed in these words: 'Forgetting those things which are behind, and reaching forth unto those things which are before, I press towards the mark for the prize of the high calling of God in Christ Jesus' (Phil. 3. 13–14).

They affirm their desire that all those Christians who belong to these two Communions may be animated by these same sentiments of respect, esteem and fraternal

117

love, and in order to help these develop to the full, they intend to inaugurate between the Roman Catholic Church and the Anglican Communion a serious dialogue which, founded on the Gospels and on the ancient common traditions, may lead to that unity in truth, for which Christ prayed.

The dialogue should include not only theological matters such as Scripture, Tradition and Liturgy, but also matters of practical difficulty felt on either side. His Holiness the Pope and His Grace the Archbishop of Canterbury are, indeed, aware that serious obstacles stand in the way of a restoration of complete communion of faith and sacramental life; nevertheless, they are of one mind in their determination to promote responsible contacts between their Communions in all those spheres of Church life where collaboration is likely to lead to a greater understanding and a deeper charity, and to strive in common to find solutions for all the great problems that face those who believe in Christ in the world of today.

Through such collaboration, by the Grace of God the Father and in the light of the Holy Spirit, may the prayer of Our Lord Jesus Christ for unity among His disciples be brought nearer to fulfilment, and with progress towards unity may there be a strengthening of peace in the world, the peace that only He can grant who gives 'the peace that passeth all understanding', together with the blessing of Almighty God, Father, Son and Holy Spirit, that it may abide with all men for ever.

✠ MICHAEL CANTUARIENSIS   PAULUS PP. VI

The Common Declaration by Pope Paul VI and the Archbishop of Canterbury

FROM THE VATICAN 29 APRIL 1977

1   After four hundred years of estrangement, it is now the third time in seventeen years that an Archbishop of Canterbury and the Pope embrace in Christian friendship in the city of Rome. Since the visit of Archbishop Ramsey eleven years have passed, and much has happened in that time to fulfil the hopes then expressed and to cause us to thank God.

2   As the Roman Catholic Church and the constituent Churches of the Anglican Communion have sought to grow in mutual understanding and Christian love, they have come to recognize, to value and to give thanks for a common faith in God our Father, in our Lord Jesus Christ, and in the Holy Spirit; our common baptism into Christ; our sharing of the Holy Scriptures, of the Apostles' and Nicene Creeds, the Chalcedonian definition, and the teaching of the Fathers; our common Christian inheritance for many centuries with its living traditions of liturgy, theology, spirituality and mission.

3   At the same time in fulfilment of the pledge of eleven years ago to 'a serious dialogue which, founded on the Gospels and on the ancient common traditions, may lead to that unity in truth, for which Christ prayed' (*Common Declaration* 1966) Anglican and Roman Catholic theologians have faced calmly and objectively the historical and doctrinal differences which have divided us. Without compromising their respective allegiances, they have addressed these problems together, and in the process they have discovered theological convergences often as unexpected as they were happy.

4   The Anglican–Roman Catholic International Commission has produced three documents: on the Eucharist, on Ministry and Ordination and on Church and Authority. We now recommend that the work it has begun be pursued, through the procedures appropriate to our respective Communions, so that both of them may be led along the path towards unity.

The moment will shortly come when the respective Authorities must evaluate the conclusions.

5   The response of both Communions to the work and fruits of theological dialogue will be measured by the practical response of the faithful to the task of restoring unity, which as the Second Vatican Council says 'involves the whole Church, faithful and clergy alike' and 'extends to everyone according to the talents of each' (*Unitatis Redintegratio*, para. 5). We rejoice that this practical response has manifested itself in so many forms of pastoral cooperation in many parts of the world; in meetings of bishops, clergy and faithful.

6   In mixed marriages between Anglicans and Roman Catholics, where the tragedy of our separation at the sacrament of union is seen most starkly, cooperation in pastoral care (*Matrimonia Mixta*, para. 14) in many places has borne fruit in increased understanding. Serious dialogue has cleared away many misconceptions and shown that we still share much that is deep-rooted in the Christian tradition and ideal of marriage, though important differences persist, particularly regarding remarriage after divorce. We are following attentively the work thus far accomplished in this dialogue by the Joint Commission on the Theology of Marriage and its Application to Mixed Marriages. It has stressed the need for fidelity and witness to the ideal of marriage, set forth in the New Testament and constantly taught in Christian

tradition. We have a common duty to defend this tradition and ideal and the moral values which derive from it.

7   All such cooperation, which must continue to grow and spread, is the true setting for continued dialogue and for the general extension and appreciation of its fruits, and so for progress towards that goal which is Christ's will—the restoration of complete communion in faith and sacramental life.

8   Our call to this is one with the sublime Christian vocation itself, which is a call to communion; as St John says, 'that which we have seen and heard we proclaim also to you, so that you may have fellowship with us; and our fellowship is with the Father and his Son Jesus Christ' (1 John 1.3). If we are to maintain progress in doctrinal convergence and move forward resolutely to the communion of mind and heart for which Christ prayed we must ponder still further his intentions in founding the Church and face courageously their requirements.

9   It is this communion with God in Christ through faith and through baptism and self-giving to Him that stands at the centre of our witness to the world, even while between us communion remains imperfect. Our divisions hinder this witness, hinder the work of Christ (*Evangelii Nuntiandi*, para. 77) but they do not close all roads we may travel together. In a spirit of prayer and of submission to God's will we must collaborate more earnestly in a 'greater common witness to Christ before the world in the very work of evangelization' (*Evangelii Nuntiandi*, ibid.). It is our desire that the means of this collaboration be sought: the increasing spiritual hunger in all parts of God's world invites us to such a common pilgrimage.

This collaboration, pursued to the limit allowed by truth and loyalty, will create the climate in which dialogue and

121

doctrinal convergence can bear fruit. While this fruit is ripening, serious obstacles remain both of the past and of recent origin. Many in both communions are asking themselves whether they have a common faith sufficient to be translated into communion of life, worship and mission. Only the communions themselves through their pastoral authorities can give that answer. When the moment comes to do so, may the answer shine through in spirit and in truth, not obscured by the enmities, the prejudices and the suspicions of the past.

10   To this we are bound to look forward and to spare no effort to bring it closer: to be baptized into Christ is to be baptized into hope—'and hope does not disappoint us because God's love has been poured into our hearts through the Holy Spirit which has been given us' (Rom. 5.5).

11   Christian hope manifests itself in prayer and action—in prudence but also in courage. We pledge ourselves and exhort the faithful of the Roman Catholic Church and of the Anglican Communion to live and work courageously in this hope of reconciliation and unity in our common Lord.

DONALD CANTUAR: PAULUS PP. VI